Always Pushing Forward

A story of goal setting and resilience
in the pursuit of the American Dream.

GAEL YONNET, M.D.

Münster   August 24 2021

Moritz,
Good luck with your studies!
Keep Pushing Forward!

Gaël

Copyright © 2019 Gael Yonnet

All rights reserved. No part of this book may be reproduced by any mechanical, photographic, or electronic process, or in the form of a phonographic recording, nor may it be stored in a retrieval system, transmitted, or otherwise be copied for public or private use – other than for "fair use" as brief quotations embodied in articles and reviews without prior written permission of the author.

ISBN: 978-1-0947-4053-9

This book is dedicated to my wife Sandra.

I do not know what the future holds but I do know that having her by my side will give me the strength and the courage to conquer all.

Foreword

By FRITJOF F. LANGELAND, M.D.

I have always been fascinated by stories of individuals who, despite tremendous personal difficulties, triumphed over them and accomplished feats that most of the human family would regard as nothing short of miraculous. These stories are well known and offer us an inspiring view into what can be done despite these personal difficulties. I think of Beethoven who composed some of the most beautiful works of classical music but never heard many of them due do deafness he suffered for the last 15 years of his life. Ernest Shackleton, the British explorer who saved his entire crew despite his ship, the Endurance, being inextricably locked and crushed in an ice flow in Antarctica in 1915. The persistence of Thomas Edison who discovered an inexpensive and practical incandescent light bulb after failing at least 1,000 times. When asked how it felt to fail 1,000 times, he said that he did not fail 1,000 times. "The light bulb was an invention with 1,000 steps." Another is the touching and inspiring story of Helen Keller, who despite being deaf and blind learns to speak and read and was the first person without sight or hearing to obtain a Bachelor of Arts degree. However, without the loving and persistent coaching of Anne Sullivan, Keller may not have emerged from her "handicap." Perhaps less well known but no less remarkable is the story of Tom Whitaker, an amputee who successfully climbed Mount Everest in 1998 after two previous failed attempts making him the first person with a "disability" to do so.

There are literally millions of less publicized accounts of individuals who accomplished truly amazing things despite hardships and roadblocks from which many of us would shrink. The single mother or father who raises children in an environment rich enough to produce highly successful and productive people is no less remarkable than the stories mentioned above. Or, I think of the bystander who comes upon an accident and somehow lifts a vehicle off a victim to save a life. Or others who intervene in cases of assault, despite personal risk, to protect those being abused. I think of the civil servants in the fire and police departments who are daily at risk and display great courage and heroism for our protection and safety. Even less well known is the mother in Africa who must walk 10 miles every day to provide water for her family. I once was invited to go fishing with a young man from Kiribati. I asked him how often he would fish. He looked at me with a blank stare and then I realized that if he did not fish, the family did not eat.

These stories, histories, are all inspiring in their own way. This book also is inspiring and where it fits in the tapestry of amazing sagas of overcoming tragedy to realize triumph, success and accomplishment is left to you the reader to decide. But for me, it is indeed an incredible account of turning tragedy into triumph. It is personal for me because I was there and experienced much of what Gael experienced as I viewed his struggles and triumphs first hand.

I was there when he arrived at the emergency department the day he suffered his terrible accident. I witnessed the severe pain he was suffering and saw the fear in his eyes when he was trying to understand what exactly had happened to him and what the uncertain future would hold.

I witnessed his battle to not just heal from the accident and the surgery physically but mentally and emotionally as well. I was thrilled to see how he slowly but surely resolved to accept his paralysis and the work it would take to develop a functionality within his "disability." I saw him get out of bed and into a chair for the first time. I helped him leave the hospital and move into his first home with the Romney's after the accident. I saw him get back to his studies in medical school and was there when he graduated and witnessed the standing ovation his classmates gave him as he received his diploma. You will see the rest of Gael's story as you read this book. It is truly a saga of triumph over tragedy.

So what is it about Gael that propelled him forward to achieve such marvelous accomplishments? Gael is a likeable individual with an engaging smile, relates well with others, hence, he makes friends easily. He is not shy and in most social situations, as well as in professional relationships, people are drawn to him. It is not surprising then that so many were willing to help him during his crisis. He is also a driven individual who will pursue a goal like a pit bull once he sets his mind on it. He plans well, he prepares well, and with his keen self-discipline he doggedly follows his plan. He is also very passionate and

I attribute this to his French heritage which gave him the stomach and the drive he needed to get through those dark tough days. Gael is also teachable. Physicians have to learn the science, the art, and the practice of medicine, and Gael had to do all this while figuring how to do it from a chair. Remember, dear reader, that ever since his accident he has always been in a chair.

I have often wondered what I would have done if placed in the same situation. It is impossible to know but my first hand witness of Dr. Yonnet's remarkable climb from tragedy to triumph has been and is inspiring. Hopefully, you will find it inspiring as well.

PREFACE

Throughout my life, especially since the accident that left me paralyzed, I haphazardly jotted down thoughts, anecdotes, key moments in my development as a human being. Never did I imagine those could be of interest to anyone. In fact, I still can't imagine how they could be. Writing things down was cathartic at times and provided an opportunity to stop, look back and reflect on the distance covered, and be grateful for the opportunities I had been fortunate to have, and for the friends I had been able to make along the way.

One day, my wife Sandra stumbled upon those random, disorganized, poorly written thoughts, and proposed that I should continue the writing of my life's story, as perhaps others could benefit from my experiences. I initially came up with soft excuses on why not to pursue the formal writing of my humble tale. "English is my second language." "I'm not a writer." "I don't have time." Despite my efforts to evade the project, over time, Sandra's casual proposition turned into a stronger suggestion, which, itself, morphed into a precise request, and ultimately, into a stern notification that the book was getting written. By that point, in spite of the outcome being inevitable, I made a final weak attempt at arguing, for good form, that my life's journey was of no interest to anyone. I was wrong, I was told, my story is inspiring, and there was no doubt in her mind that people were going to love it, as it outlines the ideology of the American Dream and the power of resilience. Therefore, I wrote this book for my loving wife, and I hope you will agree with her, and find my experiences interesting and inspiring.

INTRODUCTION

The house I grew up in was shaped like an upside-down letter L. My room was on the second floor, next to the only bathroom in the house. My parents had bought it two years before I was born. The wallpaper was typical of the early seventies and was quite psychedelic in nature. Orange geometric designs outlined in black, blue squares and yellow circles, these random patterns were the backdrop of my childhood. While the wallpaper on the second floor remains unchanged to this day, the wallpaper on the main floor was updated to an initially white textured paper in 1989, which turned into a warm hue of yellowish-brown, from decades of cigarette smoke exposure. The house witnessed the passing of the years, impassible. It saw my parents falling out of love quickly and getting divorced when I was only seven years old. It saw the doubts in the eyes of two young boys. My brother and I wondered who would care for us in the chaos. We wondered who would be steady enough to guide us through life safely. Perhaps it was up to us to find our own way, to make our own life, from scratch.

We lived in Gradignan, a suburb of Bordeaux in southwestern France. A couple of streets behind the house was a forest. The forest was rather large and seemed to me, as a youngster, to be endless. Not a day went by without me riding my bike or walking my dog in that wonderland. It was a paradise for a young boy growing up. My dog, Phebus, a handsome cocker spaniel named after a Greek God, loved the long strolls through the trees.

In the spring, the fern was so thick, in parts, that we could hike on the branches of trees and jump onto the cushioning layers formed by the wide juxtaposed leaves, to have our fall softly broken before reaching the ground. The fern was taller than I was at the time, and it was a delight to walk through it as if walking through a maze. In the summer, the trees provided a soothing refuge from the biting sun and the smothering heat. The forest was filled with chestnut trees, which, in autumn, dropped burrs of chestnuts on the ground by the thousands. I, along with every other kid in the neighborhood, would spread open the sharp burrs with my feet, and, trying not to get my fingers pricked, gathered up chestnuts so my mother could broil them in a special pan with holes at the bottom. Broiled chestnuts made a nice afternoon snack. Each season brought about a different aspect of the forest. Winter was grey and sad and it rained nearly every day. Sometimes, it rained continuously for three months and I used to wonder how much water the sky could hold. It rarely snowed, but when it did, everything stopped. It snowed briefly for the first time when I was seven years old. The next time it snowed, I was eleven. My friends and I rode our bikes through the snow, sliding everywhere. Snow was delightful for kids, who for the most part had never seen it in their lives, or so rarely. I was fortunate that my dad took me skiing each year for a week or two in the Pyrenees, and was familiar with snow, but when I saw snow at home, instead of in the mountains, it felt special and out of place. It snowed again when I was a junior in high school. Once more, everything came to a halt and our teachers allowed us to skip class. Snow was always magical to me, peaceful, beautiful and quiet. It acted as a buffer, muffling the overexcited sounds of life's mayhem. Little did I know that a violent encounter with it, would, some years later, change my life forever. For better or worse, it would be up to me to decide.

CHAPTER 1

EARLY CHILDHOOD

Initially, there were five members to our family. My parents, Yannick and Monique, my brother, David, just a year and a half older than me, our dog, Phebus and me. We ate dinner together around a foldable round table that was brought out from the kitchen and placed in front of the small television in the living room. Our parents asked us what we had learned in school and how the day went, and all was well in a seemingly perfect world. That didn't last. My parents were very different, and, in many regards, I suppose they should have never married in the first place as their union was a disaster waiting to happen. Dad was the adventurous type and always had an activity planned on the week-end. He was part of a group of people with similar interests from work. In the winter, they went skiing in the Pyrenees or the Alps, and in the summer, they went sailing in Arcachon where my dad co-owned a sailboat. Meanwhile, each week-end, Mom took David and me to our grandmother's house in Libourne, forty-five minutes away from our home. The only time we were invited to join Dad was when he went skiing for a full week while school was out, and we were all free to go. Even then, Mom never skied and stayed in the apartment all day. My mom is what is called a "Casaniere" or home-lover, someone who feels more comfortable at home than anywhere else, which was a stark contrast with my dad's enthusiasm for life and his spirit of adventure. Eventually, Dad's group started to include female friends and soon enough, he met someone who enjoyed the same outdoor activities. Dad worked nights for a newspaper. Once, Mom found a note and a phone number in Dad's jacket and that's when things started to get ugly. She called him at work and he wasn't there, so she called the number she had found in his pocket. A woman answered the phone and Mom asked if my dad was there. The woman answered in the affirmative. Mom angrily asked for the address, so she could bring Dad his belongings. Within minutes, in the middle of the night, Mom shoved David and me, along with a small suitcase full of Dad's clothes, into the car and we drove off. She cried hysterically as she drove us to Bordeaux. We circled the neighborhood in the old part of town where the buildings were dark and dismal, adding to the already depressing atmosphere. All the while, David and I sat silently, fear stricken on the back seat of the old Renault. We never found the address and eventually returned home. From that point forward, Mom cried constantly, or so it seemed. Our dad finally left us when I was seven years old. The break had been long and traumatic as he had refused to leave at first and had tried to return home on two occasions over the course of several months, prolonging the inevitable. Unfortunately, the relationship between them had degraded so badly that they had passed the point of no return. Once, he came back one evening and Mom cried and yelled and threw things at him and I woke up and walked to David's room and kneeled at his bedside. We were both afraid and said nothing. In many regards, our dad's eventual final departure from the house assuaged some of the turmoil.

Le Castel

Our local school, from kindergarten to elementary school was called "Le Castel" after the medieval castle next to which it was built. At recess, we played soccer in what used to be the courtyard of this medieval castle and, as amazing as this sounds, we took it entirely for granted, because for us, it was just the way it was, we didn't know any differently.

In the midst of my parents' divorce, the home situation was so tense at times that I found it difficult to gain the support and nurturing that I was needing as a developing child. I needed someone to be proud of me to motivate me to do well and I felt that my parents were too preoccupied with their own lives to give much thought to mine. I thus decided that if I did well in school, the adult approbation I didn't necessarily get from home, I would get at school from my teachers. That is in fact exactly what happened. I became a very good student and my teachers were proud of my efforts and their results. The fact that I did well in school gave me a sense of confidence that buoyed me for some years to come, well into junior high. When the work load became too difficult for me to excel in every single class, I would select a few classes in which the invariable aim was to make the teachers proud. I was less concerned with the actual learning than I was concerned with gaining the teachers' praise. The classes I reliably chose to excel in included biology, chemistry, French literature and English. The classes that presented more of a challenge and required relatively more effort to be successful included Spanish, mathematics and physics. When I wasn't day dreaming, riding my bike or walking my dog through the forest, I occupied my time with studying and managed to maintain good grades throughout junior high, at the end of which I sat for, and earned a "Brevet d'Education Nationale," a Diploma of National Education in French literature, history and mathematics.

That page turned, I was ready to start high school. At the end of junior high, we were asked to select a major in which to continue our studies, since, at the end of high school, and after successful completion of an extensive compulsory examination, we would be awarded a Baccalaureate in the field on which we had chosen to focus our studies. An interesting twist of fate made me select applied physics as a major, with a minor in mathematics: The two topics that required the most work. In my mind, physicists like Albert Einstein and Marie Curie were brilliant people, and I aspired to be one of them. There was only one high school offering this special program in applied physics in all of Bordeaux and it was the Lycee Alfred Kastler, named after the prominent French physicist, famous for being awarded the 1966 Nobel Prize in Physics for the discovery and development of optical methods used in the study of Hertzian resonances in atoms. I was more familiar with Einstein, but since we didn't have a Lycee Albert Einstein, Alfred Kastler would do just fine.

CHAPTER 2

ALFRED KASTLER

Most teenagers idolize pop stars and actors. I, on the other hand, admired people with brilliant minds. To me, the study of physics was unlike the study of any other academic subject, and I viewed it as one of the most interesting, even if also, coincidentally, one of the most intellectually challenging. When the opportunity arose for me to pursue a Baccalaureate of Applied Physics at the Lycee Alfred Kastler in Bordeaux, I was eager to get started.

High school, at least the one I attended, was demanding beyond belief. I was in class forty-three hours per week, took the bus at 7:21am every morning, only to return home twelve hours later, five days a week. I used to joke that, in the winter, apart from week-ends, I never saw the house in the daytime. Because of my science major, in addition to a significant amount of physics classes and all the corresponding laboratories, the major also required a lot of mathematics and chemistry. I wasn't a naturally gifted student, the kind who understands everything quickly without studying much. I always considered myself to be of average intelligence. That said, I did have a few traits working in my favor: An exemplary self-discipline and strong work ethics. Nobody studied harder or longer than I did. Whatever I lacked in intelligence, I made up for with diligence and hard work. My parents offering limited to no encouragements, it was up to me to be self-motivated.

I was in awe of people like Dr. Pierre-Gilles de Gennes, the French physicist who was awarded the 1991 Nobel Prize in Physics for his work with liquid crystals and polymers, and Dr. Georges Charpak, another French Physicist who was awarded the Nobel Prize in Physics a year later in 1992 for his invention and development of particle detectors, particularly the multiwire proportional chamber. People of uncanny intelligence had always fascinated me. Having these two French Physicists receive the Nobel Prize in Physics back-to-back within my first years in high school only strengthened my resolve to keep studying hard.

On Saturdays, I set my alarm at seven o'clock and was at my desk by eight. I worked on math problems, physics lab reports, chemistry homework. On Sundays, the same schedule would be repeated. I was studying for twenty hours per week-end. On a regular school night, I could be up until 1am studying or writing reports. My entire existence was consumed by school and studying. I even read Albert Einstein's book: "Relativity" in my down time while waiting for, or riding the bus, to and from school. My dedication and thirst for knowledge, I was hoping, would be the key to a better life.

My dad had dropped out of school when he was fourteen years old and had worked ever since for the newspaper Sud-Ouest, one of the largest newspapers in France, following in his own father's footsteps. My mom had graduated from high school but had not pursued her education further to care for my brother and me. When our dad left us, Mom had to work and had a difficult time finding jobs and was often unemployed. Unemployment was what I feared most for myself. Being educated would hopefully narrow the chances of me not being able to find a job in the future. My definition for success in life was entirely based on whether someone had a job or not, and the type of job didn't matter. I had always considered my dad to be somewhat successful because he had never been unemployed in his life. His salary did not even enter the equation when measuring success. A meager salary was better than none. My parents, it seemed, had no expectations for me, or at least none that they voiced. While I had placed expectations on myself, I was ridden with self-doubts but the harder I doubted, the harder I worked to compensate. If I worked sufficiently hard to become one of the best, success would be inevitable. I often managed to be among the top three students in my class. In 1993, when I sat for the French literature portion of the Baccalaureate which is scheduled a year ahead of all other subjects, I was Valedictorian. Another student who was reliably among the top students in the class was my good friend Xavier Gache with whom I have maintained a strong friendship throughout the years. Xavier developed a career as a sales representative for equipment used in ophthalmologic surgery.

David moved out of the house when I was a junior in high school to pursue a technical training in Libourne. The training consisted of a new concept where two weeks of school alternated with two weeks of paid work in a factory. I was very impressed that he had been able to earn money so early on. He was able to buy a cheap used car, had a girlfriend, and overall, was fully participating in life. He even bought an electric guitar and played in a rock band called Dioxine and released a CD. Meanwhile, I stayed at home with our mom and lost myself in the study of science and the reading and writing of philosophical prose and poetry. Although I had usually spent the evenings in my room each night, only to see David at the dinner table, once he was gone, I missed his presence terribly. The longer we were apart, the closer we grew.

INTRODUCTION TO RELIGION

While I was in high school, my cousin Romain, a member of the Church of Jesus Christ of Latter-Day Saints (Known over the years as the Mormon Church, or the LDS Church) was serving a religious mission in Geneva, Switzerland. While there, he had been inspired to contact the missionaries in Bordeaux and ask them to visit me.

The first missionaries who visited me were "Sisters" which is how LDS women missionaries are called. One of the them was Sister Day. Sister Day was from Orangeville, Utah. Missionaries were easily identifiable because they rode bikes around town and wore large white helmets. While wearing helmets is now quite popular and clearly the right thing to do, back then, it was not the norm and missionaries stood out like sore thumbs.

Missionary men are called Elders. Elders were always dressed in suits which was very uncommon for young men in France, and they all wore name tags. One of them told me that not infrequently, while shopping at the grocery store, customers would approach him asking where items were, as it was assumed that he worked for the store.

My aunt Francoise thought it was strange that they wore suits as she reckoned they'd be more comfortable wearing jeans and t-shirts. I told her they wore suits out of respect for the important message they were tasked to deliver. Elders were only, on average, about a year or two older than me, but the suits made them look respectable and trustworthy. Personally, when looking around at other teenagers my age, and when looking at Elders, it was clear who I wanted to emulate. Their proper attire made it easy for me to want to spend time with them and listen to their teachings. Missionaries are always in pairs, and I invited them to my home weekly for dinner. My mom was a good sport as I would often schedule dinners at the last minute and call her at work to notify her that we would be receiving missionary guests, sometimes a couple of them, sometimes four, at times six, and occasionally eight. She would have to go grocery shopping on her way home from work, and as much of an inconvenience as I imagine those last-minute shopping trips must have been, she was always supportive of my meeting with the missionaries. I think she enjoyed their company as well.

  I had no religious background whatsoever, so my religious education essentially had to start with the basics. I was interested in listening to the missionary lessons which covered topics I had never been exposed to before. They preached strong family values and the abstinence from smoking or the drinking of coffee or alcohol. I was charmed by that message which resonated true to me given the fact that my family had been broken early on, I had suffered from second-hand smoking my entire life thus far, and had witnessed how easily a nicotine addiction had held my mom hostage and dependent. I initially wasn't confident about the existence of Jesus Christ or God, but I figured it could not hurt to believe that all-powerful and omniscient beings existed and were rooting for me and watching after my well-being. French people, in general, are highly skeptical when it comes to religion and I was no exception. Believing in God, to them, is as far-fetched a concept as believing that Star Trek is real. That said, trying to believe that I wasn't alone, while it would take time, was appealing.

Over time, I met dozens of missionaries as they rotated in and out of Bordeaux while moving from city to city within the southwest region of France. Of all the missionaries, the one who spent the longest time in Bordeaux was Elder David Langeland and this prolonged exposure allowed us to develop a special friendship. To this day, David Langeland stands out in my mind as one of the most honest and trustworthy person I have ever met.

After more than a year of being visited and taught weekly by the missionaries in my home, I made the decision to get baptized in the Church of Jesus Christ of Latter-Day Saints. I had always felt at ease with the missionaries and the decision to get baptized just felt right. The baptism took place in the early part of December 1993. I didn't have a suit or any dress clothes per se, so when the missionaries asked if I needed anything prior to the baptism, I told them that I didn't have a neck tie. One of the missionaries, Elder Parker, gifted me one of his, which I still have today. After being baptized, I tried as hard as I could to attend the three-hour religious service on Sunday morning from 9am until noon, even though it meant sacrificing the time I used to dedicate to studying. I asked some of the other boys how they managed to attend Church three hours on Sundays and still get their homework done. One of them, who was studying mathematics explained that he kept a book under the sacrament table and used sacrament meeting to catch up on his school related reading. Overall, I think the academic demands placed on teenagers in France is unfathomable to most Americans who, as I understand, have a fun experience while in high school. Clearly, this wasn't the case for us.

PREPARING FOR THE FUTURE

In the last two weeks of February 1994, the Winter Olympic Games were hosted in Lillehammer, Norway. I tried to watch as much of it as I could on TV during the coinciding two-week winter vacation, and, as I saw what a true winter wonderland Norway seemed to be, I started dreaming of traveling and exploring the world.

Like most of my classmates, I was starting to make plans for life after high school. We had, as a class, toured various research centers at the University of Bordeaux, such as "Le Laboratoire d'Astrophysique" the Laboratory of Astrophysics, or "Le Centre d'Etudes Nucleaires" the Center for Nuclear Research, which was located right in my home town of Gradignan. It was during the visit to the Center for Nuclear Research that one of the young researchers explained in simple terms that they were trying to identify the elemental composition of unknown structures by shooting atoms at them, and analyzing the way the atoms bounced back. Simply put, imagine hitting a tennis ball onto an unknown structure. The degree of bounce would differ significantly whether the structure is soft, such as a piece of memory foam, or hard, like perhaps, a granite wall. Because they knew how much bounce to expect from any given element, they could deduct the composition of unknown structures based on the bounce. I was in awe at the elegance of the physics concepts I was exposed to daily, and, upon coming home from visiting the Center for Nuclear Research, I thought that it would be amazing if I could work in a field I was passionate about.

While pursuing a secondary education in physics in Bordeaux would have been the most straightforward and logical path, I still had a lot of self-doubts and wasn't sure that a secondary education was even in the cards for me, not because of my lack of funds, given that secondary education is free in France, but frankly put, because of the lack of role models or emotional support within my family. Essentially, my options appeared limited because I had always been encouraged to stay within my family's social class. My grandpa worked a humble job at the newspaper, my dad worked a modest job at the newspaper, and I was supposed to follow suit somehow. I couldn't wrap my head around what I was destined to do. Clearly, the destiny that French society had mapped out for me was incompatible with my educational aspirations. It was strongly encouraged that I not pursue any type of doctoral degree. Conceivably, as I day-dreamed of foreign travels, I could leave France altogether, to get a fresh start, somewhere entirely new, without preconceived limitations on what I could or should do with my life. Perhaps, I could think outside the box, bend the rules and find a place where I could live life to my fullest potential. Having made a lot of new friends from Salt Lake City, Utah, it seemed like a good place to explore.

I wondered about moving to Salt Lake City, but not being a resident of Utah, or not being American at all for that matter, the international student tuition at the University of Utah was thrice the regular in-state resident tuition and the resulting amount was simply inconceivable. At an Education Fair, I found the booth of a small organization which, for a fee, could make all the arrangements to get me enrolled at a Community College somewhere in Texas with which it had an affiliation. Attending a Community College, I was told, was much more cost-effective than attending a state University, and the credits earned would be transferrable to a University if I decided to continue my education in the United States after earning what would be an Associate of Science degree. I consequently asked if the organization could help me with the admission paperwork to the Salt Lake Community College instead of the Texan school. While the process would be slightly more complicated because of this change in location, it was definitely feasible. All I had to do was take the TOEFL (Test of English as a Foreign Language) to prove my proficiency in English, graduate from high school, and somehow gather enough money to sustain me overseas for the anticipated duration of my studies. I had my work cut out.

BACCALAUREATE OF APPLIED PHYSICS

In France, a comprehensive two-week long examination marks the end of high school. Each day, a four-hour test is administered in one of many subjects including mathematics, physics, chemistry, English, Spanish and philosophy. I had already sat for the examination in French literature the year before and had done very well. The remainder of the examinations would cover everything studied in class over the previous three years. Only three quarters of the pupils pass the final examination. Those who fail must redo their entire senior year before being allowed to retake the exam. Those who pass are awarded a Baccalaureate degree in their chosen field. The year was 1994, before the internet, and the list of students who passed the exam was posted on the door of the school. As I approached the door, I was overwhelmed with anxiety because I had never taken success for granted. My name beginning with the letter Y, I had only to look at the bottom of the page to see whether or not I had made the list. To my greatest joy and relief, my name was on the list. I returned home elated and proud.

As soon as school was over, I went to work as a windsurfing instructor for a month in Lacanau, a seaside town, some forty minutes from my house. The windsurfing school had allowed me to stay in a nearby campground in a small beat-up trailer. This accommodation was mediocre, but at least I had a roof over my head at night. I skateboarded on the bicycle trail to commute to and from the school and was happy to have a job on the beach. Two years prior, I had studied for and obtained a federal certification to be a windsurfing instructor and I had, prior to that, been a windsurfing student every summer while vacationing at my paternal grandparents' house in Royan. I figured teaching windsurfing could always be something I did in the summer months if all my other plans at finding a real job failed. The first lessons were at 10am and we were usually done with work by 8pm. Sometimes, I would wake up early and go surfing for a couple of hours before going to work. It was really a dreamy work environment for a teenager. Given my budding fluency in English I was assigned to communicate in English with all the foreigners, Germans for the most part. While working at the windsurfing school, I had an opportunity to meet David Frank, the French windsurfing gold medalist of the 1992

Barcelona Summer Olympic Games. I had cheered for David and had seen him win the race live on television two years prior. Life was clearly full of surprises.

Unfortunately, the sailing school notified me that they could only keep me on staff for the month of July. After that, I would have to find another job. Toward the end of July, I received a phone call informing me that the newspaper for which my dad worked was looking for temporary workers for the month of August, to replace the regular staff gone on their yearly one-month vacation. It paid nearly three times as much as what I was making at the windsurfing school. It was great news! I returned home at the end of July and started working for the newspaper on August 1st. All my life, I had been taking the bus to go to the city. This new job required me to work at night, from 10pm until 4am and buses were not running that late. I acquired a used moped for the equivalent of three hundred dollars to go to work. Initially, this used scooter worked well, but soon, it became temperamental and choked periodically before coming to an abrupt stop. Overall though, it worked well enough to get me to work on time. My duties at the newspaper factory were varied but simple. I was assigned to different stations at the end of the production line. Most often, my job was to work on the loading dock. Newspapers were wrapped together with a hard-plastic band to make bundles of fifty, allowing for easier transportation. Each bundle was tagged with a specific destination and dropped onto a conveyer belt. Trucks for each of the various cities would back up against the conveyer belt. My job, simple enough, was to stand in front of a truck and grab all the bundles tagged with the city corresponding with the truck and throw them inside. It was a physical job, but I liked it. One of the permanent workers on the conveyer belt was a man in his late fifties who could have easily passed for eighty. Life had been rough on him. He was thin, disheveled and had a long history of smoking and alcohol abuse. He was so frail that his coworkers had nicknamed him "libellule" dragonfly. He was stationed upstream from me on the conveyer belt and was drunk at work most of the time. So drunk indeed that I don't recall him doing much work at all on any given day and it amazed me that he had never gotten fired. One night, he actually tried to do some work, grabbed a bundle of newspapers, was unable to lift it off the belt, fell and was dragged on the side for several seconds before finally dropping to the ground. He just stayed there, too drunk to get up. An ambulance came to pick him up and he was taken to a drug rehab hospital and I was asked to replace him for the following two months until the end of October, while he was undergoing rehab. Because of libellule's penchant for alcohol, I had the chance to earn two extra months' worth of wages. In November, I sold all my windsurfing equipment, my surfboard, my wetsuit, all the things I cared most about at the time, all my most valuable possessions, to get the total sum of money that would make my trip to the United States possible.

Initially, I felt guilty at the thought of leaving my mom to live alone. She had been struggling with depression and I saw her as being too fragile to have to go through life unaccompanied. In the year leading to my eventual departure, I had dinner with my aunt Francoise and her husband Gerald during which I expressed my concerns. They told me unequivocally that it was not my duty, as a teenage son, to watch after my mother and that she should watch after herself, and I had to pursue my own life, no matter how far from her it would take me.

I first met Fred and Shirley Langeland, the parents of Elder David Langeland, during their trip to France at the end of his mission in the fall of 1994. They had traveled with two of their other sons, Chris and Andrew (Bubba) and came over to my house for dinner one night. Upon his return to Utah, on a Sunday, Fred had driven to the church ward near the community college where I had gained admittance, to ask local families if someone would be willing to rent me a room while I came to study. My move to America was taking shape. Elder Langeland was moving back to Utah and I would be following in a matter of weeks.

On December 21st, 1994, I turned twenty years old and a small birthday gathering was held at my aunt's house. Less than a week later, on December 27th, with two large duffel bags in which fitted everything I owned, I embarked on the plane that would take me to a new life.

CHAPTER 3

COMING TO AMERICA

For someone having never extensively traveled before, I did surprisingly well during my first trip to the United States and managed not to get lost in the multiple airports I had to transit through. I had first taken a plane from Bordeaux to Paris, a short one-hour flight to get warmed up. Then, I boarded a second plane that would take me to Cincinnati, Ohio. Finally, a third plane would take me to Salt Lake City, Utah. Three hours before our arrival to Cincinnati on the transatlantic flight, we were given custom forms to fill out. The forms contained a variety of interesting questions. Are you carrying more than ten thousand dollars in cash? I wondered if anyone had ever answered yes to that question. Another question was about race: Are you Latino, Caucasian, Islander, Native American, African American, Asian or other? The question was straightforward enough but while I knew I was white, to my surprise, white wasn't an option on the extensive list. Perhaps I should select "other." Had the questions not been printed on what appeared to be official paper, I would have thought they were a hoax meant to entertain us during the last few hours of the long flight. Am I carrying more than ten thousand dollars in cash? Is my race anything other than white? Next, they would ask me if I was hiding a garden gnome in my suitcase. I called the flight attendant over, to inquire which answer white people usually selected, since after all, the grand majority of the passengers on the plane were in fact white. He said without hesitation that I was Caucasian. I had my doubts about that answer but went ahead and selected Caucasian anyway. As far as I knew, the Caucasus was the mountain range separating the southwestern tip of Russia from Georgia and Azerbaijan, and I knew darn well that I wasn't from that region of the world. That said, I later learned that Caucasian is indeed the adjective Americans use to describe white people. I guess labeling white people "White" was either too straightforward or somehow politically incorrect, and a surrogate term, no matter how far-fetched, had to be adopted.

After landing in Cincinnati, we were welcomed by custom workers. That's when Americans were separated from everyone else. All foreigners were brought to a large room with several examination booths in front of which was drawn a red line on the floor. French people have a tendency to be untamed in public. They don't mean to be disrespectful, they were just never trained. In high school, a hallway measuring a hundred feet led to the cafeteria. The waiting line was so packed and out of control, and I was so compressed against everybody else in the melee, that I could lift my feet from the floor and be carried all the way through to the cafeteria's entrance. French people, as I had ample time to experience, have no sense of order and if they see a booth, they will maul you over to get to it first. Judging from the tone in the airport security person's voice as she verbally disciplined the first Frenchwoman who crossed over the red line while another person was already speaking to the custom agent, I figured she meant business and rules had to be followed. Another Frenchwoman tried to light a smoke while waiting, and that didn't work out well for her either, to my utmost satisfaction. We were no longer in France. A red line on the floor meant that one had to wait, smoking indoors was strictly prohibited, and above all, rules were actually enforced. It was a place of order and I appreciated that right away. Once it was my turn to speak to the custom agent at the booth, I was asked what the purpose of my visit was, and I answered that I was coming to the United States to study. I was then asked for the address at which I was planning on staying, my passport was stamped, and I entered the United States of America at 4pm on December 27th, 1994. After four more hours on a much smaller plane, I reached my final destination. I looked out the plane window and saw the lights of the entire Salt Lake valley and was startled by its size. What had I gotten myself into? How would I not get lost down there? I arrived in Salt Lake City tired but happy. Dave Langeland and his mother Shirley came to pick me up in a Toyota Land Cruiser, the largest car I had ever seen, and brought me to their house, also the largest I had ever seen. They told me to call my mom once we got home, to let her know the trip had gone well. On the phone, I briefly explained to my mom that the house was so large and clean with fine furniture and paintings on the walls that I felt I was in a museum. It was definitely a culture shock. The house I grew up in had four bedrooms, but they were all very small, and the house was always messy. My mom cleaned the house once a year and unfortunately, I initially followed suit, and my own bedroom was equally untidy. My bedroom floor was covered by notes and books to the point where it was impossible to identify the color of the carpet. Over the previous two years, I had developed the habit of cleaning the house prior to the missionaries' weekly visit for dinner. Still, the contrast between my house and the Langeland's house was sharp. There was nothing on the floor and the carpet was one inch thick and spotless.

The very first day, Dave ran me through the basics: Unlike French bills which are of different sizes and colors and easily identifiable, dollar bills are all very similar, he explained, so I must keep them organized and make sure I didn't accidentally give a $10 note when a $1 was needed. He also explained how streets were laid out. In France streets are tortuous and are identified by names only. Thus, if someone told you that they live at 9 Avenue Louis Pasteur in Paris, you wouldn't be able to find it without a map. Before Global Positioning Systems (GPS) became popular, all French people carried maps in their cars to find addresses in their own city as it is impossible for anyone to know the names of all the streets. In Salt Lake City, things were a lot easier. He explained the grid system centered around the LDS Temple. North, South, East and West, and increasing numbers when expanding outwards from the Temple. It was simple enough. In the many years I have lived in Salt Lake, I never got lost. If someone told you they lived on 1150 East and 2345 South, you'd know exactly how to get there. Another detail of importance was the fact that the sales tax, which is always included in the price tag in France, was not included in the US. Thus, I shouldn't try to buy socks costing $4.99 with a $5 bill. After Dave's introductory lesson, I knew how to orient myself in the city, how to handle money and how to buy things: I was ready to go out. That afternoon, I was brought to meet the family who offered to rent me a room in their house, right across the street from the main campus of the Salt Lake Community College.

ADVENTURES ON REDWOOD ROAD

My host family consisted of Lynn and Mike Funk and their children Heidi, Laura and Jay. They were originally from Columbus Ohio and were big Buckeye fans. They were among the finest people one could meet and were genuinely welcoming and kind.

The most notable difference between French homes and American homes is the absence of shutters on the windows. In France, all homes have either plastic or solid wood shutters to cover the windows at night. Nobody would think of going to sleep with the shutters opened. Growing up, every night before going to bed, I went outside to close the shutters and lock them from the inside. It was a habit as natural to me as brushing my teeth. It was thus quite a surprise to see that American homes didn't have shutters. To some degree, it made me feel unsafe. My window was at ground level facing the front of the house and I wondered what prevented people from walking to my window, break it to get in, and steal my belongings. Another major difference between French and American homes is the absence of a fence around them. In France, every bit of land one owns is surrounded by a fence for privacy and safety. My house in Gradignan for example, was surrounded by a 6-foot fence. In contrast, in the US, front lawns are, for the most part, fenceless. That concern about the lack of shutters and fence became especially worrisome within the first week of school. On the first day at the community college, I had met Urs, a guy from Switzerland. Urs and two of his friends, also from Switzerland, Lars and Peti, decided to go to a movie. We took a bus there, but when we came out of the theater, it was late, the bus was no longer running, and we had to walk home. In France, if two locations are on the same road, they are undoubtedly very close to one another. Take for example the famous Avenue des Champs Elysees in Paris, it is just short of 1.9 mile long. In Salt Lake, our school and the movie theater were both on Redwood Road and we had misjudged their proximity to one another. In fact, roads in the US can be very long which is a concept neither of us Europeans were familiar with. Redwood Road stretches from Bountiful to the North, to Saratoga Springs, 38 miles to the South. While the movie theater wasn't horribly far, it was still 11 city blocks away and we weren't excited about walking home given that it was dark and cold. Once we reached the level of the Salt Lake Community College, we were accosted by three guys. They spoke to Lars while four more came out of the shadows. It quickly became clear that we were not just being accosted, we were being mugged. I couldn't hear what they were asking. All I heard was Lars' answer: "No." It obviously was the wrong answer as one of the guys leaped forward and punched Lars in the face and we all started running as if our lives depended on it. In that split second between the punch and my explosive start off the starting blocks, all I saw was another guy pulling out a baseball bat. We took off so quickly that he didn't have time to take a swing, and instead, threw the bat and hit Urs in the back, but fortunately he was able to keep running. They didn't chase us, but we kept running nonetheless. The house where I stayed was the closest, so we regrouped there. Lars ended up with two broken front teeth and Urs had a sore back. I, although physically untouched, was emotionally shaken. I had been in the US for less than a week at that point and had already been mugged. On top of that, the incident happened only a block away from the house where I lived. This isolated unfortunate event taught me that some neighborhoods can be more dangerous than others and it is best to use caution when walking at night, or try to avoid it altogether. In all my ensuing years in the US, I was never mugged again.

CHAPTER 4

SALT LAKE COMMUNITY COLLEGE

The first classes I took as I enrolled at the Salt Lake Community College (SLCC) were English as a Second Language (ESL), developmental reading and composition, and mathematics. I had planned on taking math initially because of its universal language. I figured even if I didn't understand anything the teacher said in the classroom because of the language barrier, I would still be able to do well because of my strong background in the field. Indeed, I excelled and achieved very high grades in mathematics, exam after exam. The teacher wrote the name of the highest scorer for each examination on the board, and my name remained on the board the entire quarter. This fueled my confidence. I was very proud of myself and was off to a great start!

The other two classes had for goal to enhance my proficiency in English. The developmental reading and composition class was quite reminiscent of the philosophy classes I had taken in France. We read articles on various topics and wrote responses. I enjoyed these exercises very much as they allowed me to develop my ability to write down my thoughts. The ESL class was taught by Kathy McIntyre. The class, as one might expect, included only foreign students for whom English was a second language. The class focused on improving our listening comprehension skills and our speaking ability. The majority of the students were from Asia, namely Japan and Korea. Besides me, there was only one other student from Europe and it was Urs Lichsteiner, my Swiss friend. Urs came to Utah to snowboard in the Wasatch mountains and had decided to take the ESL class to improve his English. In fact, he didn't even have a student visa and was only in Utah for less than three months on a tourist visa. Urs and I went snowboarding each and every Saturday. He also went on Sunday, but I attended Church instead. Urs was a good friend to me. Kathy and I, because we shared a love for the mountains, quickly became friends beyond the classroom. She and her husband Ross had a cabin near Solitude up Big Cottonwood Canyon, and invited me there on several occasions. They also were gracious enough to take a lot of pictures of me snowboarding, which allowed me to create a nice portfolio that eventually led to me getting sponsored. Kathy, Ross and I have remained friends to this day. As an interesting anecdote, the United States earned 13 medals atced Winter Olympic Games in Lillehammer, Norway which I had watched extensively on TV, and Ross' sister, Elizabeth McIntyre had brought home the silver medal in Freestyle skiing, Women's moguls.

ENGLISH AS A SECOND LANGUAGE

I had been exposed to people from different countries and different cultures while in high school, but having met them in my own country meant that I didn't learn as much about their culture as they learned about mine. The LDS missionaries of course were mostly from the United States, and I had some other friends from Germany, Norway, Sweden and Denmark who had come to France to study French at the University of Bordeaux. The ESL class at the SLCC, beyond helping me with my English, also exposed me to people from Asia for the first time. I remember an episode where we were asked to speak to the class about our country through the description of a particular experience of our choice. A male student from Korea spoke about his mandatory military service in Korea and teared up as he described the physical punishments he was subjected to while in the military. It was an experience nobody could relate to or even fathom and in that sense, while heartbreaking, it was truly peculiar and interesting. The Japanese folks talked about a popular game they often played and which I had never heard of before. I forgot exactly what it was, but I reckon it was some variation of dominoes. I only remember that they were very fond of it. It was very thought-provoking to see that the way of life I was accustomed to was not "the norm" but just one of many. While it was not its original intent, the ESL class truly broadened my mind. The following quarter, I elected to take an Anthropology class in order to further learn about other world cultures like the Inuits or the Pygmies and their respective belief systems and interests.

While in high school, I had started to study Vovinam Viet Vo Dao, a Vietnamese martial art which I practiced quite intently for three years. Once in Salt Lake, I realized that several sports and physical activities could be learned in designated classes from the school. College credits could even be earned. What a superb idea! I therefore enrolled in Tai Chi and Kung Fu classes and from then on, I tried to enroll in physical education classes whenever I was in school as it provided balance to my schedule.

In France, whether it be in high school or at the University, curriculums are set in stone and there is no choice in what classes can be taken, when or from whom. In the US, I could select whatever class I wanted and choose the days and times on which it would be taught as well as the person teaching the class. I tremendously loved the freedom the American way provided. Another striking difference was the relationship with the teachers. In France, there is a strong barrier between the teachers and the pupils. All the pupils stood at attention when the teacher came in and said "Hello" in unison and essentially, we were mostly scared of teachers. In the US, teachers provide their personal contact information as part of the syllabus and are very friendly and approachable. I personally think that it is a better approach to education.

The other classes I took during my second quarter at the community college included American history, art history, astronomy and geometry. I took classes in anything I had an interest in and had never been exposed to before or topics I wanted to revisit out of shear fun, and it was an exciting time and a wonderful opportunity to study whatever I wanted.

I didn't go to school in the summer following my first two quarters at the community college, and instead, had a chance to travel all over the western United States.

A Transcontinental Journey

In June 1995, my aunt Marielle and five of her friends landed in Salt Lake City to start a self-guided tour of the western states. It was an unexpected and golden opportunity to see Utah, Nevada, California and Arizona. I jumped on the band wagon, or, more accurately on the blue Ford Econovan, as we traveled for three weeks. Marielle was a seasoned traveler and had used a book to plan the entire trip. The book had full itineraries laid out, including where to stay and even recommended where to eat per budget categories. The first night was spent in Winnemucca, Nevada, and the second, in Reno, The Biggest Little City in the World. We visited nearby Virginia City and its Victorian buildings from the 19th century mining boom and worked our way across the Pass to Lake Tahoe. I completely fell in love with the place. It was so beautiful, and the water was so clear. It was fascinating to me, to see that one could snow ski in the morning and water ski in the afternoon, in the same stunning scenery. We camped near the south side of the lake on the California side. We then traveled through Sacramento on our way to San Francisco. We set camp in the Muir Woods National forest north of Sausalito in a campsite surrounded by giant redwood trees. I was really impressed by San Francisco, having only seen its streets on the big screen. We hit all the main touristy spots, from the Golden Gate Bridge to Coit Tower, Castro, TransAmerica tower which I guess isn't a hot tourist ticket but was interesting to us nonetheless because of its unusual architecture, Pier 39, Chinatown, Japanese Gardens, the famous Lombard Street and even rode in a cable car. We also drove to multiple view points on the golden gate bridge and I took many beautiful pictures. The one aspect of life in San Francisco that is the most breathtaking, is the parking situation. I have never seen cars parked on streets at a 45-degree incline. I suppose none of the streets are actually that steep but let's just say that they look steep enough and I am glad I never personally had to drive and park on them.

We eventually left for Los Angeles and stopped by Santa Cruz, Monterey, Carmel, Santa Barbara, Malibu and Santa Monica along the way. My aunt's book listed interesting facts about each location. Thus, we learned that Carmel was famous for having had Clint Eastwood as its mayor. As we came close to Los Angeles, I was quite surprised to find a beautiful campground right in Malibu, overseeing the Pacific Ocean. Los Angeles was also phenomenal to me. I felt very fortunate to have the opportunity to visit this renowned city and to walk on Hollywood boulevard. Again, I regaled in taking pictures of famous actors' stars and of the Hollywood sign up on the hill. We even drove through Beverly Hills and took pictures of the mansions like the true tourists that we were. We then made way to Las Vegas and onward to the Grand Canyon. We took a plane's ride in the canyon which was quite a unique experience. The flat light from the towering sun and the subsequent lack of shadows and contrast, made it difficult for me to appreciate the full depth of the canyon. We thus decided to wake up at sunrise to see the canyon while the sun was low and rising, and it was a marvelous sight to behold. We also took a horseback ride on the canyon rim. We then drove toward Monument Valley on the Navajo reservation and stopped in Page at the south tip of Lake Powell, to visit the dam. Something interesting caught my attention in Page. On the main road, dozens of different churches were lined up right next to one another.

The Church of Christ, the Church of God, the Church of the Father and the Son, the Holy Church, it just kept going. The creativity in some of those names was astonishing. Of course, I was rather new to religion and in France, we basically only knew about the Catholic Church and the Protestant Church, and of course I knew of the Mormon Church since it was my denomination. But in Page, on that single street, they had churches I obviously had never heard of, and that I suspect exist only there. As we neared Monument Valley, many shops were situated on the side of the road where Navajo families sold gorgeous handcrafted silver jewelry. The campground was set right in front of the Mittens made famous in John Ford's Westerns with John Wayne. When I was eight or nine years old, one of the French television networks featured Westerns on Tuesday nights. We often drove to my aunt's apartment to watch those with her and that's how I became familiar with John Ford's pictures shot in Monument Valley. While I didn't remember any of the storylines, I did remember the Mittens. Again, I woke up early to take in the sight as the sun rose over this awe-inspiring place. I felt peaceful, isolated, as if this pristine place was detached from the rest of the world. The next day, we took a guided jeep tour in the valley and a Navajo woman explained the name they had given to all the different rocks because of their shapes. The Thumb, the Three Sisters, the Totem Pole. She also sang a song in Navajo inside a large cave. Finally, we visited many of Utah's stunning National Parks including Bryce Canyon, the Needles district, Canyonlands, and Arches. I was overtaken with admiration at the grandeur of the Delicate Arch and the vibrant red rock in Bryce. I had never seen anything of the sort before. Basically, the entire trip was breathtaking. It was a fun packed three weeks, and was without a doubt, the best vacation I ever had.

In the first week of July, a few days after I came back to Salt Lake City, the Funks invited me on a road trip to Columbus, Ohio to visit their extended family. They planned on stopping to see a variety of attractions along the way. Having just visited many western states, I couldn't pass this opportunity to travel to the Midwest and jumped on that wagon as well. We first drove north to Yellowstone. There, I saw Old faithful from which, as expected, spurted out gallons of steaming hot water, a hundred feet into the air, at reliable time intervals. The water was so hot indeed that it evaporated on the way down before touching the ground. We also saw a plethora of natural springs which edges were lined with colorful rings making them look like effervescent rainbows. We then made way toward Rapid City, South Dakota and visited Mount Rushmore National Memorial in the Blackhills National forest. How they were able to sculpt those grandiose faces with dynamite, in the side of the mountain, is beyond my understanding. On a nearby mountain, they also had, sculpted in the rock, the face of a Native American. This unfinished monument was called Crazy Horse Memorial. Still in South Dakota, in a town called De Smet, we visited the Laura Ingalls Wilder Historic Park. I knew Laura Ingalls from the television series: The Little House on the Prairie, which aired in France when I was growing up. From there we drove to Minneapolis and stopped at the Mall of America, which, I was told, was the largest mall in America, or at least, it was the largest at the time. It was so large that a full amusement park fitted inside. We then went to Chicago and finally reached Columbus. Columbus was noticeable for its smothering humid heat. I felt as if no air was getting in my lungs when trying to inhale deeply. It was a peculiar sensation that I'll never forget.

Overall, I visited twenty-six states during my first few months in the United States and had the chance to see many amazing sites and attractions.

Having ran out of money upon my return from this extensive trip, I had to return to France in September 1995. It was a strange feeling to return home after having experienced all the things I had experienced that year. I had a single goal in mind: To go back. I quickly found a job in a surf shop and worked there until February 1996 by which time I had saved enough money to afford the trip back to Salt Lake City and one quarter worth of tuition. I jumped on a plane and started school again in April. Initially, I was allowed to stay at the home of Paola Franco's parents. Paola was a friend I had met in the language tutoring lab at the Salt Lake Community College where I volunteered to help students who were studying French. Frida and Carlos Franco let me stay in their home until I found a place to rent closer to campus. In exchange for their help, I assisted Carlos with errands for his used car dealership during the day before going to school in the late afternoon. I was very grateful for their help. The support provided by Frida and Carlos allowed for my story to continue.

Within a few months, I was able to move in the basement of a house in sugarhouse, a cute neighborhood in South Salt Lake. I lived for about a year in this small house a few blocks from the Salt Lake Community College south city campus. Two other people lived in the house. The room I rented for $250 a month was in the basement and was very rudimentary. There were two small windows, one of which was broken. I nailed a blanket over it to prevent the cold from coming in during the winter months and my dog Digger, a Labrador-Retriever mix I had adopted at the Humane Society, slept in the bed with me to keep me warm. I had very little money left after paying rent and my school tuition, and I survived mostly on cereal. I lost fifteen pounds in a short time secondary to this limited diet. These were the harshest living circumstances I ever encountered. While it would have been easy to give up and return to France to live with my mom, this was not an option I considered. I didn't expect my new start in the US to be easy, but I hoped the effort and sacrifices would pay off in the long run, so I put my head down and persevered, one day at a time.

A Growing Interest in Medicine

Some of the classes I selected denoted a growing interest in medicine and included anatomy, physiology and medical terminology. As a foreign student I did not have authorization to hold a regular job in the United States. To earn some money, I helped out people with various manual labors such as car washing or yard work. I also ran errands and tutored kids with their physics, chemistry and mathematics homework for a small hourly fee and somehow managed to get by. One day, I heard of a cooperative student work program that was available through Salt Lake Community College. It allowed foreign students to gain exposure to the work environment while earning school credits. All I needed to do was find a job in the industry in which I was hoping to work in the future. At the time, no matter how unrealistic it appeared, I had dreams of working in the medical field.

Dr. Fred Langeland, after discussing how well I was doing in school, inquired what type of career I was hoping to pursue. I answered that a job in a medical lab would likely suit me well since I was interested in medicine. He asked why, if my interest was in medicine, I wouldn't pursue a career as a physician. I didn't know what to answer. A career in medicine was undoubtedly out of my league, I thought, and hadn't spent any time contemplating it as an option. From experience, the only friends I had in France who had pursued medical studies were sons and daughters of physicians or lawyers. These were smart people from wealthy and influential families who were essentially predisposed to such careers. I didn't belong in that group. My paternal uncle Patrice came from a humble family and had somehow gone to medical school, but he was clearly the exception to the rule. None of his parents or siblings had gone to college and few had graduated from high school. My own family was modest, and I figured I had no business attempting a career in medicine, even though my rigorous, disciplined study habits had earned me a 4.0 GPA. Fred, however, encouraged me to consider going to medical school as a viable option. He said: "You're in America now, and you can pursue any career of your choice, and you are clearly smart enough for medicine if that is what you want to do." Once, as Shirley and I were visiting with one of her neighbors in front of her house, the neighbor asked what my educational plans were. I answered that I had decided to eventually go to medical school. The neighbor replied: "You need to be smart for that." I was too shy to say anything and Shirley replied: "He is absolutely, without a doubt, smart enough for medical school." Never before had I experienced that kind of support. Having them believe in me, allowed me to believe in myself. While I was used to hearing my name spoken by my own parents in negative terms my entire childhood, it felt like an empowering contrast to hear my name spoken by Fred and Shirley in glowing terms that made me feel special, able, and gave me confidence.

HEMODIALYSIS

As part of the cooperative education program, I was allowed to be employed in a field related to my career aspirations, and as a consequence of my newborn ambitions with regard to medical school, I went to LDS hospital under Fred's advice, to speak with a Human Resources (HR) representative and explained that I was looking for a job in the medical arena to gain exposure to the field. The HR representative said they were looking for a dialysis technician in one of the outpatient dialysis centers. I had no idea what a dialysis technician did, but the idea of getting a real job in a clinical setting sounded terrific, no matter what it was. I bought a three-piece suit too big for me at the Deseret Industries thrift store and met with the outpatient dialysis manager for an interview. His name was Larry. Luckily, he agreed to give me the job. I underwent in-house training for several weeks. Initially, my duties included cleaning the dialysis chairs and machines between patients with hydrogen peroxide to wipe off whatever blood might have dripped during the treatment, rinse the dialyzers and attach the prescribed potassium concentration baths to the back of the machine for each patient. A few months later, I was promoted and learned to hook up patients onto the dialysis machine and monitor the treatment. The patients were all in end stage renal disease, most often from diabetic nephropathy. I inserted large bore needles into arteriovenous fistulas or implanted GoreTex grafts in the patient's forearms. The blood would flow from the patient to the dialyzer that would act as an artificial kidney, remove the unwanted toxins and balance the blood's electrolytes. The neat thing about dialysis was that the inventor of the artificial kidney, Willem Johan Kolff had been the head of the University of Utah's Division of Artificial Organs and Institute for Biomedical Engineering where he was involved in the development of the artificial heart with Robert Jarvik. I loved this job. It made me feel important. I was assigned to certain patients and would see them for three to four hours every other day which allowed for the creation of great rapport. The hours were long, usually from 5am until 4pm but they enabled me to go to school in the evening. My classes were from 5pm until 10pm most nights. After school, I would get home, eat a bowl of cereals and go to bed to rise the next morning at 4am. I had very little free time to study and was exhausted most of the time but continued to do well in my classes nonetheless.

One day, an elderly gentleman nicknamed Flash came in for dialysis. He was a new patient and lived only a few blocks down the road in a nursing home. His kidneys had failed him, and he wasn't really looking forward to the ongoing dialysis treatments but had agreed to give it a whirl. Flash was a tall, healthy looking man in his late eighties. When doing my initial assessment on him I asked how his vision was and he started reading the small numbers on the screen of the dialysis machine on the other side of the room. I turned around and could barely read them myself. He was in good health apart from his kidney failure which exceptionally, was not secondary to diabetes. Flash had received his nickname after Flash Gordon because he was so fast on the basketball court in his youth. I dearly enjoyed my regular visits with him and was fond of all the stories he told. He had eight decades' worth of stories to tell, each more interesting to me than the previous one. After I had shared with him my goal of becoming a physician but also my concerns regarding how difficult it was to gain acceptance to medical school, he taught me to think outside the box. He said that often there were several ways to reach the same goal. Two of his sons, he explained, were physicians, and both were practicing in Utah. One had gone to school in the United States and the other, having failed to gain acceptance in one of the US medical schools had traveled to Mexico, learned Spanish and had enrolled in a Mexican medical school. After obtaining his medical degree from Mexico he returned stateside, took the boards and was now practicing locally. Two different paths leading to the same result. If it is important to you, he said, you'll find a way.

On a spring afternoon, after the dialysis treatment, Flash quietly told me that he had decided to stop dialysis. He had lived a good life, his wife had passed away a few years prior and he was ready to be with her again. He had discussed his plan with his nephrologist and was planning on eating a lot of tomatoes and bananas and let his serum potassium rise. The electrolyte imbalance would, in a few days, make him fall asleep and die serenely. It was the first time I sat face to face with a friend, knowing that he would no longer be around in a matter of days. My first instinct was to beg him to reconsider. I didn't. I couldn't. It wasn't my place. He had calmly explained that it was time. He was at peace. I respected his choice, no matter how much it hurt. I accompanied him to the parking lot where I gave him a hug. We both wept during the long embrace. He told me that things would be ok. It was the last time I saw Flash. When I came back inside, the tears in my eyes made it difficult for me to program the dialysis machine for the next patient. One of the nurses noticed and said to me: "Get used to death kid, it happens around here." I never did get used to it. Flash died fifteen days later.

A Significant Turn of Events

The owner of the house my roommates and I were renting, who had been living overseas, came back to live in the house and we were asked to move out. I didn't have anywhere to go. Fred and Shirley still had all their kids living at home and couldn't reasonably take me on. I didn't know where to move to. I drove around looking for a room to rent to no avail. I couldn't find anything within my meager means. Eventually, I thought of putting up an ad in Church one Sunday morning to see if anyone would be interested in renting me a room in their home. That's when I got yet another break that allowed me to push forward. Jana Rees called me the next day while I was at school to give me her address and invite me to come up to visit her and her husband. Jana and Dr. Bill Rees, a general surgeon in Salt Lake City, lived in a sumptuous home in Federal Pointe, a gated community. I had no idea that such communities even existed. I stopped at a gate, called in, and they remotely opened the gate for me and I drove up to their house. For the next two hours, I had the feeling of being in a movie, completely detached from reality. Everything about the house was spectacular. It was perched on the hill, was beautifully designed and had a large pool overlooking the city. The entrance was wide, made of stone and down a few steps, was an indoor fountain with a bronze statue of a child holding a kite below a big sun well through the ceiling. It was a stark contrast from the basement room I was living in. After a short discussion with Jana and Bill,

Jana said that I was welcomed to stay with them and showed me the room that would be mine. I couldn't believe my eyes. The room was more like a luxury suite than a room. I had never seen anything like it. I didn't know they made beds that big. Adjacent to the room were a walk-in closet and a private bathroom with a tub. All those rooms had motion sensor switches and the light turned on automatically whenever one walked in. Two of the four walls were lined with oversized windows offering the most astonishing view of the pool and the Salk Lake valley. Helicopters flying in and out of the University of Utah Hospital actually flew below us. It was an unbelievable upgrade from my basement room with the broken window and these new accommodations allowed me to comfortably continue my work in dialysis as well as my studies. Jana, Bill and their whole family were the most wholesome people. They effortlessly incorporated me in their family and made me feel like I belonged. Upon discussing my educational plans with Jana and Bill, I explained that I had decided "to try" to go to medical school after Fred and Shirley Langeland had encouraged me to pursue such an avenue. Jana immediately placed an empty glass on the table in front of me and handed a water pitcher and asked me "to try" to fill up the glass. I filled up the glass. She then said: "You see, there is no trying, you either do it or you don't, if your mind is set on doing something in life, you just do it, that's the American way." Bill added that getting accepted to medical school was no easy task for anyone, but he believed that with my work and study ethics, I would be successful in reaching my goals if I kept my head up and continued to work hard. I graduated from the community college with honors in April 1998, at which time I was summoned to return to France by the French Government to undergo a mandatory military training.

CHAPTER 5

MILITARY SERVICE

I was flown back to France, courtesy of the French Government, in June 1998. My military training was set to start in October, which left me with the whole summer to try to find a job and earn some money. I was fortunate to find temporary employment at a factory for the group Schneider for which my brother worked. Schneider built large electrical appliances. My job consisted of standing outside the oven that cooked the powder coating on the metallic casing of these electrical appliances and retrieve those burning items with leather gloves to place them on storage racks. The pieces were extremely hot and, as I grabbed them, the heat quickly penetrated through the thick gloves. The large items were difficult to handle and often touched my bare arms, leaving me with multiple burn marks. Of course, while standing next to an oven might have been nice in the winter, I stood there in the peak of summer when the outside temperature was already greater than 90 degrees Fahrenheit with a high humidity level, making the job very uncomfortable overall. I never did complain. After all, a job meant money in the bank which allowed me to pay off a used 1992 Geo Metro I had bought in Salt Lake City a year before. The summer passed quickly and soon, the time came for me to join the army. At that time, in France, it was every young man's duty to serve their country for ten months. I worked at the factory all the way until a few days preceding my enrollment into training camp.

I had received instructions in the mail according to which I was to take a train to the city of Agen where an army bus would await to take me to the military base. There were many young men waiting to board this early train and I presumed that we were all going to Agen for the same reason. A few conversations were started on the train. We were going to basic training, but we were scared as though we were going to the slaughter house. We had no idea what to expect.

Upon arriving in Agen, it was immediately obvious that we had lost our personal freedom. "Walk this way! Stop! Wait here until we call your name! Come here! Sit there!" Every movement we made was the result of an order. We were brought directly to a clinic where we had to give a urine sample and receive several immunizations.

We were then taken to the cafeteria for lunch and the food was good and varied. As far as I knew, it was the same food I had always eaten throughout my entire education in the French school system. The one good element about meals that have been created for tens of thousands of people in a government run cafeteria system is that they are always well balanced and nutritious. After all, we were in France and the French take their food seriously. That meal was the first down time we had the whole day and it was short lived.

After lunch, we were taken to a warehouse to be fitted with leather boots, army fatigues and a beret, after which we went to the barbershop. The barber needed no specific training for the job at hand. All he had to do was grab a pair of electric clippers and shave our heads.

Once our heads were buzzed, we were shown our dormitories. The rules were strict. The beds had to be made in a very precise way. The upper sheet had to come twenty centimeters from the top of the bed before being folded back over a blanket. The fold itself had to measure ten centimeters. The entire bed had to be tight and creaseless. After a quick demonstration, we were told to do our own beds. An overzealous power-hungry sergeant checked all the measurements with the help of a pack of cigarettes as a measuring tool. Any slight variation from the demonstrated version resulted in the mattress being violently thrown across the room with the sheets ripped off mid-air. Of course, this theatrical event was accompanied by a soundtrack consisting of a lot of yelling and cursing and we were ordered to do the bed over until it met the hormonally imbalanced sergeant's expectations.

A Tight Schedule

Lights were out at 10pm nightly, no exceptions. A loud bell rang at 5am daily to wake us up. We then had thirty minutes to shower, shave, get dressed and wait in line in the front of the building. There, the sergeant would walk through the ranks to inspect us. He carried a piece of paper and scraped it below our chins to see how close shaven we were. If it wasn't close enough, even though we had just shaved, we were yelled at and ordered to shave again. We then walked to the cafeteria, only a few buildings away on the military campus and were ordered to stay put, standing to order until the cafeteria opened at 7:30am which meant we stood immobile for close to two hours. We were asked to wear the summer fatigue which consisted of a light shirt with rolled up sleeves, even though we were then in October and the mornings were quite chilly. If it rained, it made no difference; we stood still, soaked, for hours, waiting for the cafeteria to open. Of course, it was their way to break our spirits down and establish their authority over us and teach us discipline. One day, a higher ranked officer walked by and saw us all wet and cold. He got angry and asked the sergeant if he was trying to get us all sick. Later that day, we were told to transition to the winter outfit which consisted of a long-sleeved shirt and a wool sweater. I was allowed to keep the wool sweater when I left the military and still own it today. It is green with my name velcroed on the left chest.

We purposefully had not been told how long the basic training was supposed to last. It was another way for them to mess with our heads. The mornings were usually spent learning about various military topics which I found very interesting. We were taught about the firing power of the French assault rifle and how to take it apart to clean it and how to put it back together quickly. We also learned that the main reasoning behind having a strong nuclear arsenal was to dissuade other nations from engaging us in a conflict. In the afternoon, we would either walk in formation, run to exercise, or go to the firing range to practice shooting.

Walking in formation was a real drag. First, we were all lined up based on our heights. The tallest person was placed on the front row on the left side. His name was Cyril Cavero and he was 6'7". The next tallest person was placed on his right side and so on. After six people filled the front row, a second row was started. Being fairly short at 5'8", I was standing on the last row toward the middle. After being neatly organized, we were taught to walk in unison by all striking our left heel on the ground simultaneously. We were also taught military songs to help us keep the same walking rhythm. While I do not remember the lyrics to any of the songs, I do remember that one was titled "Ceux du Liban" Those of Lebanon. Once, as we were learning the lyrics to a song, we were asked if any among us had a good singing voice so we could help the others to sing in tune. I was eager to volunteer my voice which sounded in tune to me. Within a few verses, it was evident that the sergeants were not in agreement with my self-evaluation. "Were you joking? Go back to the middle of the group, NOW!" I guess I wouldn't have qualified for American Idol. When walking, the leading sergeant would yell "Droite!" or "Gauche!" depending on whether we had to turn right or left. We had to repeat the command as loud as we could and execute it, starting with the front row that took the lead to initiate the turns as the rest of the group followed. Unfortunately, the second tallest guy, Henry, fairly consistently turned the wrong way, and each time he messed up earned us another trip around campus as a punishment. We weren't sure why he had such a hard time with his right and left, but it soon became evident that the poor guy didn't do it on purpose. After a few mistakes, we assumed that the sergeant would cut him some slack and let us go to bed. We were mistaken. As we were the last group to still circle campus after the night had fallen, it was clear that we either had to do it right as a group or keep walking around together, as a consequence for a single member among us getting the order wrong. It was all about team effort. We asked the two guys on either side of Henry to grab his arms and lead the way for him. It was an easy solution and eventually everyone was allowed to go to bed.

Aside from all the yelling, the lack of personal freedom and the overall feeling of being a prisoner, boot camp was really fun.

Our army files contained everything about our skills and education. On my file, I had mentioned that I had worked in hemodialysis and was skilled in providing such treatments. As it turned out, the other five guys I was rooming with, all had a special training that could be used in a healthcare setting. Two guys were radiology technicians, two were physical therapists and one was a laboratory technician. Only ten days after arriving in Agen, all my roommates plus some guys from other groups were moved to Bordeaux to be assigned to work in the "Hopital des Armees Robert Picque" the Robert Picque Military Hospital. Meanwhile, the others continued basic training in Agen. Having grown up in Bordeaux, I was given the choice to either room with others in the military dorms adjacent to the hospital, or live in my mother's house. I of course opted to live at home. The Army would provide all my meals and I was given a $100 a month stipend.

CHAPTER 6

HOPITAL DES ARMEES

Upon my arrival at Robert Picque, by chance if you want to call it that, I was assigned to work with "Professeur Jacques Bahuaud" a world-famous orthopedic surgeon, General 3 stars in the French Army and recipient of The Legion of Honor. An intake interview was set up, during which he learned that I had been living in Salt Lake City. He mentioned having traveled to The Orthopedic Specialty Hospital in Salt Lake to work with Drs. Lonnie Paulos and Thomas Rosenberg on a new surgical technique to repair torn anterior cruciate ligaments called the double looped semitendinosus and gracilis autograft method, developed by Dr. Leo Pinczewski of Sydney Australia with whom he had also worked. Out of sheer luck and unfunded association, he exclaimed that these surgeons were meticulous and conscientious, and he had no doubt I would be the same and he welcomed me into his inner professional circle as his trainee with a loosely defined role. Having this extraordinary man volunteer to be my mentor was another defining moment. Over the ensuing months, he took me under his wing, provided education with respect to orthopedic surgery, encouragement with regard to my budding education, and protection in the form of exemption from some of the, what he called "chronophage" or time-wasting activities the structured military training would require of me, in favor of what he felt were more constructive activities by his side. Consequently, from working so closely with him each and every day, I became second author on multiple research endeavors which proved to be of incredible value in the pursuit of my medical education and subsequent career progression.

Dr. Bahuaud gave me a desk in the little room adjacent to his office and assigned me to the creation of educational brochures for surgical patients. These brochures were aimed at telling people about all the different surgeries offered within the department. It detailed how the conditions were diagnosed, how they were treated and what could be expected from the surgery. I learned much about orthopedic procedures during that time. I also acquired a new level of proficiency with computers having to work on the creation of illustrations and the layout of the brochures.

While under Dr. Bahuaud's tutelage, I occupied myself with a variety of projects and was trained to assist in surgery. As a result, I became quite efficient at helping with knee replacements and anterior cruciate ligament (ACL) reconstructions. Dr. Bahuaud used the double looped semitendinosus and gracilis tendons technique, also known as the hamstring technique. At the time in 1998, this technique was revolutionary and only very few surgeons in the world used it. Dr. Bahuaud had learned it directly from Dr. Leo Pincewski in Sydney, Australia. Dr. Bahuaud was always involved in cutting edge surgical procedures. Another procedure he brought to France and helped study was the autologous chondrocyte implantation for the treatment of cartilage defects.

Hyalin cartilage, unlike other biological tissue, is largely unable to heal itself secondary to its avascularity. Cartilage defects in the knee had been notorious for leaving countless people with severe pain and significant disability. As early as 1981, Dr. Lars Peterson from Gothenburg, Sweden showed that it was possible to grow rabbit cartilage in vitro. In 1987, Dr. Peterson and his team did the first human cartilage implantation. Dr. Bahuaud adopted the technique in 1996.

The procedure was simple enough, in theory. The first step was to take a biopsy of the lesion under arthroscopy, a technique by which scopes and instruments are inserted inside the knee via little holes made through the skin. Once the biopsy made, the cartilage sample was placed in a saline solution and sent to the laboratory of Genzyme Tissue Repair in Boston, Massachusetts. There, under a complex process, the chondrocytes were isolated and placed on a specially engineered culture medium. Their growth was allowed to take place for up to 21 days after which period the chondrocytes had multiplied by a factor of ten. The new chondrocytes were sent back for implantation. This time, an arthrotomy, open surgery, was necessary. The edges of the cartilage lesion were prepared in very much the same way a gardener cleans the edges of a lawn with a shovel around a flower bed. Then, a piece of periosteum, the tissue covering the bone, was taken from the tibia and sutured and made waterproof over the lesion, thus creating a pocket ready to receive the chrondrocytes which were then injected with a syringe. Six weeks later, on arthroscopic follow-up, the lesions appeared beautifully repaired with hyaline-like cartilage.

The surgical suite was state of the art with a remote-controlled video camera attached to the ceiling over the surgical site. Sometimes, I would entertain visiting surgeons in a conference room. From there, I was able to control the camera, zoom on the areas of interest and overall, explained the different surgical steps in progress on the screen. Via an audio interface, we, in the conference room, were able to communicate at any time with the surgeons. These video sessions were highly educational. At other times, bovine knees were brought to us to practice the surgical procedures and I was able to perform other cartilage repair techniques such as microfracturing and mosaic plasty.

Of course, the involvement in cutting edge procedures meant being implicated in research. All the results from the ACL plasties using the hamstring technique and the autologous chondrocyte implantations had to be documented, analyzed and presented. Often, during surgery, I would take pictures to document what we were doing, and I also drew schematics pertaining to the surgeries, to be used as illustrations either on posters or in medical publications.

While I worked with Dr. Bahuaud, he traveled all over the world to present the results of these innovative techniques. I was very proud to be involved in such work. Dr. Bahuaud entrusted me with a lot of responsibilities which really boosted my confidence. Then, more than ever, I was set on a career in medicine and no obstacle could stand in my way.

I made very little money, but the knowledge I acquired was invaluable. At the end of my year of military service, Dr. Bahuaud wrote me letters of recommendations which helped me gain acceptance into Brigham Young

University and later, the University of Utah School of Medicine.

I applied to Brigham Young University to get a bachelor's degree and complete all the pre-med requirements. Following my acceptance to the school, I traveled back to Salt Lake City in December 1999 to continue my studies.

CHAPTER 7
BRIGHAM YOUNG UNIVERSITY

On December 1999, I flew back to Salt Lake City to embark on the next chapter of my life. I had been accepted to Brigham Young University in Provo, Utah. Emil, Fred Langeland's brother and next-door neighbor and his wife Diane knocked on the door the night before I left for college and handed me a massive box full of food. The support I was fortunate to get from everyone was unbelievable. It was as if the universe was working in my favor and everybody in my vicinity did what they could to help me along. The first time I drove down to Provo, I had to find my way to the University and managed to get lost in a neighborhood. I got out of the car and asked a man where BYU was located. He pointed in the direction of campus and said: "Well, if you had kept driving around, sooner or later, you would have landed on campus, it's hard to miss." At the Wilkinson student center, I grabbed a brochure which listed all the BYU approved housing complexes and found an apartment with five roommates, whom I had never met before. Most students were having a good time, enjoying what is often referred to as "college life." Not me. I was on a mission to succeed. I wasn't there to enjoy myself, I was there to study and get results. I was dedicated to being successful in a way that was not conducive to a thriving social life. I enrolled in pre-med classes and soon focused on the field of Neuroscience. I would wake up at 5:30am in the morning, shower, shave and be on campus studying by 6:30am even though my first classes didn't start until 8am. If I needed a quick nap during the day, I would lay down in a hallway or under a table in the library for a 15-minute power nap before getting right back to studying. I would stay in the library until midnight daily. I was a machine, albeit, an exhausted one. After my initial semester, my grades were such that I qualified for a scholarship that covered half my tuition in the Fall and Winter semesters, and all my tuition in the Spring and Summer semesters. Once I had a chance to get the lay of the land, I slowed down just a little and incorporated in my day, activities other than pure studying. From 11am until noon, I would work out and lift weights. I met Cedric Moran in the gym and consistently worked out with him. Cedric was born of an American father and a French mother. We also happened to have a few classes in common and often studied together. He was a good friend. After the daily work-out I would eat a warm lunch. Grandpa John Langeland had insisted on paying for a meal plan each semester so that I could have access to a balanced nutrition and not go hungry. Eventually, I was hired as the French living resident at the BYU Foreign Language Student Residence (FLSR) which was a small apartment complex where students could live to accelerate their learning of a foreign language through an immersion program with a native speaker. One of the requirements of the job was obviously to speak French with the other 5 roommates and to cook and eat dinner with them daily to provide them with consistent exposure to the language they were learning. My roommates at various times in the French apartment included Juan Pablo Heinz, Rex Biggers,

Jon Jensen, Jason Wheeler, Sterling Jensen, Jonathan Osterlund and Adam Charles and we are still somewhat connected thanks to Facebook. Aside from French apartments for both men and women, the BYU FLSR had apartments dedicated to German, Spanish, Portuguese, Italian and Arabic. Interestingly enough, I recently looked up the languages offered and found out that Italian had been dropped and the complex now offered Russian, American Sign Language, Japanese, Chinese and Korean and that the languages offered varied upon student demand. I made a lot of friends there.

While walking to and from campus, I read self-improvement books such as the famous "How to Make Friends and Influence People" by Dale Carnegie, or inspiring books such as "Gifted Hands" by Dr. Ben Carson. I was loving life. I was fitter, wiser and better educated than I had ever been before. In the course of my studies I had the chance to develop a few meaningful friendships which endured over the years, namely with Jayson Smith who became a pediatric dentist in Bristol, Tennessee, Brad Rand who became a dentist in Brewer Maine, Jason Sotto who became a dentist in Winter Garden Florida, Wayne Mortenson who became a radiologist in Boise, Idaho, and Ben Romney who became a radiologist in Salt Lake City, Utah. I also had a very close friend named Dawn Ruesch with whom I took a lot of pre-medical classes, and who eventually became a pharmaceutical sales representative for Pfizer. She married, had two boys and unfortunately, a decade after graduation, while in her mid-thirties, she passed away after a courageous battle with cancer. The news of her passing came as a significant shock to me and made me realize how fragile life can be.

A Tactical Approach to Education

For the most part, the classes I took at BYU were familiar to me. There was a lot of chemistry, mathematics, physics, molecular biology, psychology, and I excelled essentially in everything, with one exception: Organic chemistry. Organic chemistry was entirely new to me and was a beast of a topic. Many students thought of organic chemistry as plain brutal. Consequently, I scheduled it, along with its associated lab, in the spring, when I was carrying a lighter overall credit load, and could focus almost exclusively on it. Scheduling classes wisely was half the battle at being successful in college. Taking all the easy classes together in one semester, and all the hard classes together in another semester, is not advisable. Mixing the various degrees of difficulty was essential. I listed all the classes I needed to complete to meet pre-medical and graduation requirements, and prioritized them in the order they needed to be completed, and estimated which ones would be more challenging than others. I then devised a master plan. Also, I always incorporated physical education classes in my schedule in order to attain not only intellectual growth, but physical wellness as well. A healthy mind in a healthy body. I took classes in weight-lifting, stretching and diving, which were very enlightening and relaxing. Physics was the topic in which I did particularly well and ended up with the third highest grade in a class of 150 students. There were a lot of very bright people at BYU, and probably the smartest guy I met there was Ben Romney, who crushed every single class. There are people so gifted that success comes to them naturally, and he was definitely one of them. He is the son of Ann and Mitt Romney. Ben was an avid skier, and, as his father was organizing the 2002 Salt Lake City Winter Olympic

Games, we spent many week-ends at the family cabin in Park City. Ben ended up being the flag bearer for the French Athletic delegation in the opening ceremony. While I was unable to attend the actual ceremony, Ben had invited me to the rehearsal which was a beautiful, awe-inspiring show that artfully retraced the history of Utah. During the course of the Olympics, I had the opportunity to attend a few events. My friend Scott Calder invited me to see the Men's downhill in Park City and had gifted me tickets to the medal ceremony and Goo Goo Dolls concert at the Olympic Medals Plaza. I also had invited Dawn to see a Women's Ice Hockey game between China and Finland at the Peaks Ice Arena in Provo. It was so nice to be a part of this wonderful and uniting experience. Who would have thought that eight years after watching the Olympics in Lillehammer, I would partake in the experience first-hand in Salt Lake City. Life, clearly, continued to be full of surprises.

A Top Notch Faculty

The faculty at BYU was of the highest quality, with each faculty member being an expert contributor in their field. My chemistry professor, for example, Daniel L. Simmons was the discoverer of the cyclooxygenase-2 (COX-2) enzyme that is the target of celecoxib and other COX-2 inhibitors which are a type of nonsteroidal anti-inflammatory drug used extensively in the management of inflammation and pain. Target selectivity for COX-2 was valuable in the reduction of peptic ulceration, a side effect of less selective nonsteroidal anti-inflammatory therapies.

While at BYU, I had the opportunity to meet very interesting and distinguished people as they visited campus to lecture. One of those was Richard D. King, President of Rotary International who gave an inspirational account of his path to success in the practice of law, and the pursuit of public service and humanitarian endeavors. His story was deeply motivational and highlighted the need to not only seek excellence in whatever one was doing, but to also focus on serving others. There are endless benefits that come from helping others, and the person who perhaps benefits the most from helping others is the person providing the help. Stop and think about that for a minute. The person who benefits the most from serving others is not the recipient, but the person providing the help. These words would set me on a life-long journey to always seek ways to help others.

Another distinguished speaker was Dr. William D. Phillips, recipient of the 1997 Nobel Prize in Physics together with two other physicists, Steven Chu and Claude Cohen-Tannudji, for their contributions to laser cooling. Dr. Phillips was especially recognized for his invention of the Zeeman decelerator which is an apparatus that is commonly used in quantum optics to cool a beam of atoms from room temperature to within a few Nano Kelvins, one hundred million times cooler than liquid nitrogen, which itself, is so cold, at 77 degrees Kelvin, that it boils at room temperature. I invite anyone to look up some of his lectures on YouTube. During his lecture, he explained in easy to understand terms what his life's work was all about. I was both enlightened and amazed that someone of such exceptional intellectual ability could communicate so effortlessly with a crowd, and simplify incredibly complex conceptual ideas, so they could be understood by almost any audience. He provided clear metaphors and examples which allowed for these mathematically difficult physics notions to be grasped. Ever since, whenever faced with a complex theory, I always try to think of how I could explain it to a novice. I call this the art of simplification. Development of this skill would prove handy in the future. As fate would have it, Dr. Phillips commented to me during our after-lecture chat around a Levitron, the antigravity magnetic spinning top which he used as a prop, that Alfred Kastler had been the first to come up with the concept of Lumino Refrigeration, or, in other terms, the use of lasers to cool atoms by way of slowing them down.

Why should we care about slowing down atoms? In a nutshell, slowing down atoms improves the accuracy of atomic clocks, and the more accurate atomic clocks are, the better the Global Positioning System (GPS) Satellites, which utilize atomic clocks, can accurately provide information with regards to our location, to the navigation systems in our cars. Therefore, in a way, whenever you use the navigation in your car, you are directly benefitting from the slowing down of atoms via the use of lasers.

MODELING

To earn money, I was permitted to work on Campus, and one day, out of the blue, a woman approached me to ask if I would be interested in modeling for the Art Department. The requirement for the job was easy, one had to possess a speedo and a high level of confidence to have one's body scrutinized from every angle. All I needed was a speedo. And just like that, I was hired. Before my very first session, I thought it would probably be best if I came with a little tan since everybody looks better with a tan. I therefore laid in a tanning bed for perhaps 25 minutes the day before, which is absolutely not advisable for so many health reasons. I turned up to my first 3hr session red as a lobster. It wasn't a great look. Essentially, the students would decide what position I would be in and used tape to mark the platform or the chair so that I could resume the exact pose after my short breaks initially every 15 minutes. Staying in the same position for 15 minutes in a row, as easy as it may sound, is in fact quite difficult in nature. Knowing that one cannot move, for some reason, gives one the urge to move. Muscles get ankylosed and achy. Eventually, I built up enough stamina to be able to remain immobile for 45 minutes between rest breaks. I sat or stood on a raised platform in many different art classes so that dozens over dozens of students could paint, draw, or sculpt my image for about a year. During the sessions, we either played music or a CD of Jerry Seinfeld's special: "I'm telling you for the last time." I heard that one-hour stand-up routine so often that I had the whole monologue memorized. Some of the students did exquisite renditions of my image and I sure wish I could have kept some of the paintings and sculptures that were created, as a souvenir of the time when I was fit. In particular, a young woman sculpted a bust, and looking at it was like looking in the mirror. This bust must be somewhere in an attic collecting dust. About a year later, while I lived in Salt Lake City, someone I had never met before, approached me to say that they had just gone to a Graduation Art Show at BYU, and there were paintings and sculptures of me all over the gallery. That's the funny bit, obviously, even though I never truly thought of it specifically at the time, there are a lot of paintings of me wearing a speedo floating around.

Eventually I was also hired as a model and actor for the Missionary Training Center (MTC) of the LDS Church in Provo. My role was as a French Mormon Missionary and the videos were aimed at teaching French through the depiction of various common situations missionaries could encounter. Again, perhaps five years later, someone asked me if by chance I was the actor in the MTC French videos. I was only recognized once and as much as I would have liked the attention, was never bothered by paparazzi.

MEDICAL SCHOOL APPLICATION

I did quite a bit of volunteer work while at BYU, mainly as an English-French interpreter, and also for the Missionary Training Center. Listening to a language while concurrently translating and speaking in a different language in a microphone requires a tremendous level of concentration which had to be maintained for up to an hour at a time. I really enjoyed this activity and always felt at peace in the company of missionaries. In a way, it was missionaries who had opened the door to new opportunities in my life and it was nice to, in turn, do whatever I could to help them out. It was during this volunteering that I met Andelyne who served a mission in Geneva Switzerland and the eastern portion of France prior to returning home and marrying my friend Ben Romney.

About a year and a half prior to the start of medical school is when I started preparing my application. The competition when applying to medical school is so fierce that the rejection rate can be quite high, even for noteworthy applicants with amazing GPAs and Medical College Admission Test (MCAT) scores. It was consequently recommended by the Pre-Med Advisement Center at BYU to apply to a dozen schools and be prepared for rejection. Before sending my official application, I decided to make an appointment with the Director of Admission at the University of Utah School of Medicine (SOM). Certainly, I could have gotten all the answers to the questions I had about the admission requirements to medical school from books, as there were plenty on the topic, but I figured nothing could beat a face-to-face meeting. Everybody I met in the admissions' office was very kind and helpful in the preparation of my application. In particular, Kathy Doulis and Goldie Kacinski were tremendously supportive and encouraging.

The University of Utah School of Medicine was the first to invite me to interview in the Fall of 2001. At the end of the interview process, the attending physician directing the interview asked me if I had applied to other schools. I replied that indeed, I had been advised to do so. She then asked: "Hypothetically, if you were guaranteed acceptance to the University of Utah, would you still interview with the other schools on your list?" I said that I wouldn't, as the University of Utah was my primary choice. She then said: "I think we are done then, I have no further questions." I came home from the full day of interviews and Fred asked me how it went. I replied that I was pretty sure I had been "hypothetically" offered a spot in the incoming class. Indeed, in January 2002, I received the confirmation letter that I would be starting medical school at the University of Utah in August. I was over the moon with this news. My hard work was paying off. I was among the first students to be notified of their acceptance to medical school that year, and it gave me an uncanny sense of accomplishment. Because of my early acceptance, the Pre-Med Advisor asked me if I would help select and prepare the next batch of pre-med students from BYU. My job was to review their academic profiles, GPA, MCAT scores, their letters of motivation, their letters of recommendation, evaluate their breadth of experiences and interests in life, and finally interview them, after which I summarized all the information and gave my personal recommendation in the form of a cover letter. I always asked the students I interviewed to teach me something in which they were skilled, knowledgeable or proficient. It was interesting to see what answers this sort of open request would yield. One student taught me how to create diamond patterns in the lawn when mowing. Another taught me how to prepare for a marathon. I genuinely enjoyed this work, learned a tremendous amount from interviewing others, and appreciated the opportunity to coach deserving students toward their dreams of becoming physicians. To this day, Brigham Young University is one of the top feeder schools to medical schools across the country.

I graduated from BYU in June 2002 with a Bachelor of Science with an emphasis in Neuroscience when at the time, BYU's Neuroscience program was ranked 6th in the country. I went back to France for a one-month vacation in July and returned to Utah in August to attend the graduation ceremony and start medical school the very next week.

CHAPTER 8

MEDICAL SCHOOL

While at BYU, I spent most of my time away from school at Fred and Shirley's house. They had become the template on which I was hoping to base my new life. They had a wonderful marriage and, as individuals, were wholesome and embodied all the values I knew made people exceptionally great. They had perfect integrity and immaculate ethics and were an excellent example to me. They were also devoted, supportive and loving parents to their children. It is often said that we cannot choose our family, we can only choose our friends. I bent the rules and added them to my family and always refer to them as my American parents. When I moved from Provo to Salt Lake City for medical school, it was obvious that I would move-in with them.

Medical school started off with a white coat ceremony at Kingsbury Hall during which, as one might expect, white coats were gifted to medical students as a sign of our entrance into the medical field. Fred, Shirley and Dawn attended the ceremony. Fred and Shirley gifted me a beautiful black Doctor's bag, and I was elated and could hardly believe that I had achieved this important goal I had set out for myself. Simply getting into medical school, I thought, was an achievement in itself. Of course, it was only the beginning of an intense period.

During the ceremony, I met Dr. William Close, a physician with one of the most eclectic medical careers anyone could have. We hit it off initially due to his proficiency in the French language which he had learned while living in France during his youth. Eventually, he enrolled as an undergraduate student at Harvard University. His studies were put on hold during the second world war when he served as a pilot in the United States Air Force. Following the war, he enrolled in medical school at Columbia University. One thing led to another and, as I recall, before finishing his surgical residency in New York, he moved to the Democratic Republic of the Congo in Africa where he became the personal physician of President Mobutu Sese Seko and Surgeon General of the Nation's Army. After a few years, amidst disagreements with Mobutu's politics, Dr. Close returned to the United States where he became a rural physician in Big Piney, Wyoming. That is where he still resided when we met. He wrote several books that I all recommend, among which, a fascinating account of his life titled: "A Doctor's Life: Unique Stories." He wrote another thought-provoking book about the transformation of modern healthcare into a business, titled: "Subversion of Trust." He was a calm, gentle giant of a man and an infinite repository of insight, knowledge and wisdom. We shared the love of dogs and the outdoors and would communicate with one another from time to time over the ensuing few years. He invited me to come visit him in Big Piney but unfortunately, something always got in the way.

Drinking from a Fire Hose

During the first week of medical school, we were told that studying Medicine was like drinking from a firehose and that over the next decade, new research findings would render half of the information learned either incorrect or irrelevant, but we didn't know which half. We were essentially sitting for an examination every other week. The firehose analogy was appropriate as the amount of information thrown at us daily was nothing short of mind-blowing. Classes were mainly held in the morning, from 8am until noon, and the afternoons were set aside for independent studies. Early on, we were asked to identify medical specialties of interest so that we could be paired with mentors. Because of my exposure to it, I was interested in orthopedic surgery, but other specialties were also of interest to me for a variety of reasons. Plastic surgery was appealing to my artistic sense, neurology and neurosurgery were appealing because of my undergraduate studies in neuroscience and the life story of Dr. Ben Carson. I won the lottery when Dr. David Renner, a young and vibrant attending neurologist, was assigned to be my mentor. The program was simple: To gain exposure to whatever field we had chosen, through the shadowing of our mentors during their clinical work one afternoon per week for five weeks. I started shadowing Dr. Renner in his neurology clinic at the University of Utah Hospital. The diagnosis of certain neurological diseases can be very challenging, and the amount of detective work involved in the process is nothing short of an art and fascinated me. Dr. Renner was quite simply a gifted clinician and I felt privileged to have the opportunity to learn directly from watching him interact with patients, perform a perfect, comprehensive neurological examination, derive a logical diagnosis, answer the patients' questions and formulate a treatment plan. He was excellent at every aspect of patient care. At the end of the five weeks, I didn't feel like telling Dr. Renner that my time with him was up, and instead, continued to shadow him in his clinic at the University Hospital or the George E. Wahlen VA Medical Center, one afternoon per week for the next two years.

At the beginning of medical school, I was introduced to Brooks Rohlen from the class ahead of me, as he was assigned to be my student mentor. Once again, I lucked out. Brooks is a charismatic, energetic and talented individual who had taken upon himself to use his financial wealth to improve people's lives through the creation of the Charity Smith Memorial Foundation. Each year, he organized a fundraiser called "The Green Tie Dinner." The first Green Tie Dinner I attended was held at The Pointe restaurant on top of the Huntsman Cancer Institute, which Brooks had reserved for the evening. The purpose of the event was to raise money by selling plates to the dinner, but Brooks was so generous that he allowed medical students to attend free of charge. Essentially, he floated the whole event out of his own pocket. The following year, I wanted to help and volunteered to put on a show at the dinner. Brooks had reserved a private reception hall at the Grand America Hotel where the dinner would be served. We decided that it would be funny if I presented a completely bogus "3D light show extraordinaire" and sold 3D paper glasses to the guests, which I could autograph for an additional donation. As the show started, we took a picture of the entire gathering of people wearing their 3D paper glasses while staring at 2D pictures of a road, pokemons, a telephone and a chair. People tried to adjust their glasses, flipping them around trying to understand why the 3D effect was failing. The message was simple: The real value of contributions to a Charity is not the show, or the food, it is in the knowledge that as a group, we were able to generate funds that would ameliorate other people's lives. The following year, the dinner was held in a colossal reception room at the Fremont Hotel in San Francisco. Brooks, a few other people and I, had opted to drive together in Brooks' truck from Salt Lake City to San Francisco. Given the distance, we made the trip in two days and stopped one night in Truckee, California where we were hosted at the house of Brooks' friends Tim and Holly McGowan. Tim and Holly own and operate Perennial Nursery in Tahoe Vista and have the most amazing home perched atop a hill overlooking Donner Lake. They are both delightful. Tim is an avid outdoorsman and Holly, who lives with paraplegia, enjoys cross country sit-skiing. It was a chance encounter and our friendship would grow stronger over time.

ADMINISTRATIVE DUTIES

The first year of medical school, Elizabeth Johnson and I were elected Co-presidents of the freshman class by our classmates and were required to participate in various administrative meetings.

In the anatomy lab, we had to dissect corpses to familiarize ourselves with proper human anatomy, which can differ greatly in appearance from the beautifully colored drawings or computer-generated images that could be found on the pages of anatomy books. Obviously, the corpses that were used were from people who had passed and donated their bodies to science. One afternoon, we were notified that a ceremonious interment for all the people who had died and donated their bodies to science would take place at the Salt Lake City Cemetery. I put on a black suit, jumped on my scooter and drove a quarter of a mile from home to the cemetery. There, I found out that the local TV network had sent a news anchor to report on the event. At some point in the ceremony, the pulpit was opened for those who wished to make some remarks in front of the families of the donors. Being as afraid of public speaking as anybody else, the thought of making impromptu remarks, from the pulpit, at the funeral service of twenty-five people I had never met, in front of their loved ones, didn't even cross my mind. Yet, as no one approached the pulpit, the pressure grew more palpable. I looked up to see people staring at me and heard someone whisper: "You are the Co-President of the class, you need to say something." I went up, stricken with fear, and tried as best as I could to deliver a respectful, grateful and heartfelt message to the audience. The message, in reality, probably sounded weak. I had not yet mastered the art of public speaking. I was embarrassed and vowed to learn the art of eloquence and be ready to make off-the-cuff remarks whenever necessary in the future.

Medical school was not only intellectually challenging, it was emotionally challenging as well. For the first time in a long time, I was no longer an exceptional student compared to my peers, but was just part of the norm. The explanation for this is quite simple. While I might have ranked 3rd out of 150 students in my physics class at BYU, technically speaking, only the top 7 students made it to medical school, meaning that I was no longer 3rd out of 150, but really 3rd out of 7 in my new surroundings. This essentially left me ranked in the 40s out of 102 students. I wasn't comfortable sitting in the mid-tier of the class and became very depressed over it. Over time, I realized that, in the midst of excellent students, sitting in the mid-tier wasn't so dramatic after all, even though it had damaged my ego a little bit. As I mentioned before, I didn't consider myself to be especially intelligent, but my work ethics and dedication had always buoyed me through nicely. In medical school however, my abilities really got tested and I occasionally wondered if I would be able to pull it off.

SUMMER RESEARCH

During the summer between the first and second year in medical school, I received a scholarship to carry out a research project and reached out to my fellow Frenchman, Dr. Jean-Marc Lalouel, a distinguished Howard Hughes Medical Institute investigator and geneticist at the University of Utah, to temporarily join his team. There, I had the chance to work with Dr. Barbu Gociman, a physician by training, who is among the smartest people I have ever met. Dr. Gociman is one of those gifted people who understand everything at a level unconceivable to most. When I say I worked with him, that is a bit of a stretch and it would be more accurate to say that I followed him around the lab like a puppy and was overall more a hindrance to him than anything else. He would often say: "Why don't you take a long lunch, go to the pool or something?" Clearly, he got a lot more work done when I wasn't around. Dr. Gociman was very kind and helped me put together a research poster titled "Role of Systemic and Renal Angiotensinogen Overexpression in the Pathophysiology of Hypertension" which I had the opportunity to display at The Ninth Annual University of Utah Frank Tyler Fall Medical Student Research Symposium in the Deer Valley Lodge in Park City, Utah. Dr. Gociman, after earning a PhD in Genetics at the University of Utah, continued his medical training and is now a fellowship-trained board-certified plastic surgeon specializing in all areas of craniofacial surgery including cleft lip, nose and palate deformities, craniosynostosis, and ear reconstruction, as well as general pediatric plastic surgery, post-traumatic facial reconstruction, and all aspects of aesthetic surgery.

Next to Lalouel's laboratory in the George & Dolores Eccles Institute of Human Genetics, was the laboratory of a titan of genetic research and a man with a most phenomenal personal history. Dr. Mario R. Cappechi was born in Verona, Italy in 1937. Between four and eight years of age, the circumstances of his life led him to become a homeless child, after his Italian father, Luciano, an airman, had been reported missing in action, and his mother, American-born Lucy Ramberg had been sent to Dachau Concentration Camp in Germany. After his mother's release from Dachau, she was able, by some miracle, to reconnect with her only son, and the two of them moved to the United States in 1946. While I invite anyone interested to research the details of this extraordinary man's life on their own, it can be said that he joined the laboratory of James D. Watson, co-discoverer of the structure of DNA at Harvard University, and after receiving a Ph.D. in Biophysics in 1967, he joined the faculty at the University of Utah in 1973 where he continued to work for the remainder of his celebrated career.

In 2007, Dr. Mario R. Cappechi shared the Nobel Prize in Physiology or Medicine with Sir Martin J. Evans and Oliver Smithies for their discoveries of principles for introducing specific gene modifications in mice using embryonic stem cells. That technology is widely known in scientific circles as "gene knockout technology" or "knockout mice" in which a specific gene can be turned off, providing endless applications in the field of genetic research.

At the end of the first two years of medical school, I stacked up all the power point lectures that we had been exposed to in class, and it reached higher than my personal height of 5'8". Never had I thought I would read so much in such a short amount of time.

Edonis & Calypso

In October 2004, while walking through a pet store, I saw four teenagers around the rabbit exhibit. As I approached, I heard them say to the rabbit "You better eat well now because we'll put you in a carboard box in the garage and won't feed you." I quickly found the salesperson and told him that I would adopt the rabbit to save her from the boys. I named this beautiful Dutch rabbit Edonis. She had a gorgeous white and gray coat. While I let her roam free through my bedroom during the day, I placed her in her large cage at night as I was initially worried I could inadvertently hurt her in my sleep if she slept on the bed with me. After a year, I had her spayed as was recommended by the veterinarian, and after the surgery, by fear of hurting her tender belly by picking her up due to the incision, I let her sleep outside the cage and eventually threw away the cage altogether. I spent a lot of time on the floor with Edonis while studying and we grew very attached to one another. She was following me around everywhere. When I was in bed, laying face down on a pillow, she would jump up on the bed and bundle up against my cheek until her nose was touching mine. Because the clinical rotations required me to be away for long hours during the day, I decided to get a second rabbit so they could provide each other company and adopted little Calypso, a Dwarf Hotot rabbit with a fully white coat. Calypso was a shy little girl, much smaller in size than Edonis and together, they were absolutely adorable.

The last two years in medical school were dedicated to clinical rotations. Each rotation was 6 weeks in length, during which students gained exposure to a specific medical specialty, one after another. I can't really say that I enjoyed that part of my education because we were expected to work extremely long hours, which wasn't anything new per se, but by that time, I was becoming genuinely exhausted. I looked forward to my six-week vacation and had made sure to schedule it in the winter so that I could use the time to study for the Medical Boards, snowboard every day, and maybe catch up on my sleep a little bit.

As fate would have it, while the second half of the senior year in medical school can occasionally be laid back, mine would be harder than anyone could have anticipated.

CHAPTER 9

THE SNOWBOARDING CONTEST

Snowboarding was a big part of my life. I had been sponsored by Ride Snowboards and Arnette Optics after my first winter in Salt Lake City, and later, by Caution Snowboards and Smith Optics. I snowboarded every chance I had. It was almost silly, juvenile, as if I had never grown up. At 31 years of age, I was still a student with a rather hectic schedule, lived at Fred and Shirley's home and snowboarded for fun and relaxation. I took six weeks off each year in my third and fourth years of medical school to prepare for the first two steps of the National Medical Boards, and concurrently went snowboarding every single day for at least two hours as a break from studying.

I would usually wake up early each morning and study hard until noon. I would then eat a light lunch before driving up to Brighton resort to snowboard a little and get my mind off the books. I would then return home, drive my scooter to the Fieldhouse, the large gym for the University of Utah student body. There, a cardio workout with an elliptical machine awaited me. My knees and ankles were much too damaged by years of snowboarding to allow me to run on a regular treadmill. My left knee made a clearly audible click each time I bent it while weight bearing, and it could not be extended past 170 degrees. After 500 calories burnt on average in thirty minutes on the elliptical, I continued the routine with weightlifting exercises until the end of the hour. I would then return home, shower, eat dinner and study again until 1am. I was undoubtedly in the best shape of my life.

2006 was going to be a key year. I was set to graduate from medical school and was hoping to start a residency program in neurology at the University of Utah.

During the last two weeks of February 2006, the Winter Olympic Games were held in Torino, Italy. Once again, my love for the Olympics was rekindled and I closely followed the results of this international competition. In fact, I was so enthralled by the Olympic spirit, that I thought it could be fun if I entered a competition myself and enrolled in a snowboarding contest from the US Snowboarding Association. It would be entertaining, and a nice way to turn the page on my life pertaining to snowboarding, to focus more intently on the next chapter: My budding medical career. As it turned out, my entire life book almost got slammed shut in the process.

On March 3rd, 2006, I went up to Brighton ski resort to practice jumping off snow-built ramps called kickers, and only stayed an hour on the hill not to tire myself. The competition was set for the next day.

When I arrived home, a letter was waiting for me. It was the notification that I had passed the second step of the National Medical Boards. At that very moment in time, my happiness knew no bounds. The board examinations had always intimidated me. It now belonged to the past, and I would cruise along gently until graduation from medical school, which was approaching quickly. Having passed those two dreadful tests, USMLE part one and two, nothing would be standing in the way of me obtaining an M.D.

Fred took me to dinner to celebrate, and I called Dr. David Renner to tell him the good news about the boards. I told him I would be entering a contest the next day and asked if he would be interested in coming up to see me compete. He replied that he was on call at the hospital and wouldn't be able to come. That night, when we returned from dinner, I prepared my equipment. The hip guard, the upper body armor, the helmet, the knee pads and tibia protectors. Everything was nicely laid out. With so much protective gear, one might have thought me bulletproof. Diane David was the only one of my friends coming to see me compete and she had agreed to film the contest. My camcorder was fully charged, my board was waxed, I was ready to go. I woke up early on Saturday morning in order to get to Snowbird ski resort to confirm my registration before doing a few practice runs at the expert slopestyle park. I met up with Diane in the parking lot at the base of the canyon, and soon, we were on our way up little cottonwood canyon. I registered and signed the contract stating that I understood the danger involved in this type of competition during which I could sustain severe bodily injuries or even death. All I really read was "blablabla." I bought my pass at 7:41am. Diane and I then walked the long path to the location of the contest. She waited at the bottom of the park in an area where some metal rails had been placed for sliding on, as is common in a slopestyle course.

It had snowed quite a bit overnight, and after taking a long lift up, I enjoyed one of the best powder runs of my life on my way toward the park. My legs were burning. The organizers waited to open the course, and I only had time to do a single practice run. There were three jumps in total; The first one had two ramps, one placed 20ft and the other placed 30ft from the landing. The second jump was a flat pyramid tabletop measuring 40ft. Finally, the last jump had three possible ramps ranging from 30ft to 40ft from the landing. They were all of different shapes and lengths but were all mighty and scary-looking. I remembered the rule of thumb: Speed checks don't bounce! I needed to go fast enough to reach the steep landing area. Failing to do so, one might run the risk of landing on the flat tabletop portion which is never good. So down I went, straight, to gather as much speed as possible, and clear all the jumps. I can't say that I fully identified which of the ramps I was launching from and didn't really adjust my speed to the different lengths. I figured that more speed could not hurt, and the faster the better. On my first run, all went well until the last jump. I jumped so high that I was barely able to stick the landing. There was yet another possible run to take. Not needing to do it, but wanting to, for the sake of the video Diane was filming at my request, I went back up and dropped in again. On the last jump, I opted for the left ramp, the closest to Diane, hoping for a better video angle. I came down too fast, went up too high, and while in the air, looking down, way down, I knew the landing would be difficult and painful. Interestingly enough, I actually had time to think to myself that I would likely break my legs on impact. I stayed in the air so long that I completely cleared the landing area and landed in the flatter zone at the base. I have no recollection of how I landed exactly. From what I heard people say, I rotated forward and crashed on my upper back. I lost consciousness very briefly and when I came to, the same song that I had selected when I dropped in was still in my earphones: AFI girl's not grey. A few people were already around me, including a ski patrolman telling me not to move. I had crashed hard before, this certainly was nothing new. The patrolman asked me the date and time and I replied: "Saturday March 4th, 2006, 11am." I knew he had to ask, I knew the routine, and I knew exactly where I was, there was no reason to worry, I didn't have a concussion and I felt absolutely no pain. He added that things would be alright: The helicopter was already en route. That new piece of information immediately concerned me. How did I fall to make them think I needed a helicopter to life flight me to the hospital? Had the full body armor I was wearing with high density articulated spine protection not been able to soften the crash? My buttocks felt numb and cold, and I assumed it was from sitting in the snow too long, so I tried to move around. Instantly, I realized something was wrong. My attempt to move my body was in vain. I was unable to lift my chest from the snow and was unable to move my legs.

I reached under my clothes with my left hand, touched around my stomach and realized that I couldn't feel anything. It was as if I was touching somebody else. I could only feel through my hand below the belly button. I immediately knew the meaning of this quick examination; I had injured my spinal cord around the tenth thoracic vertebra. Fear was upon me. I looked around and saw Diane, asked her to call Fred to tell him what had happened. I then closed my eyes in an effort to escape the situation and was loaded in the helicopter. While in the air, I requested that my friend David Renner be called and informed of my condition. I asked what hospital I was being transported to, looked out the helicopter's window briefly and closed my eyes again. Interestingly, my thoughts were occupied by worries regarding my medical student loans. I was heavily in debt. How could I ever repay these loans if I was paralyzed? Could I ever get a job from a wheelchair that would give me an income sufficient to afford the payments? What would my life be like in a wheelchair? Was the injury to my spinal cord something that could be surgically repaired? The answers would come, in time.

When we arrived at the University Hospital a few minutes later, I was freezing, and pain was starting to creep up my back and grow in intensity. As I was rolled through the ER entrance, I quickly looked around, saw Fred and closed my eyes again. The trauma team cut up my clothes as well as my protective gear and ordered multiple imaging studies. I kept my eyes closed the entire time, in an effort, again, to separate myself as much as possible from the most horrifying experience I ever had to live through, up to that point. I still vividly remember the tremendous amount of pain I experienced as I was transferred into the different imaging devices. I felt awfully cold and shivering only made the pain worse. I had some plain films, an MRI and a CT scan of the head and spine. Dr. Renner reviewed the images quickly and rushed to see me. I trusted he would tell me the truth, and I asked what my chances to ever walk again were. "I'm afraid your spinal cord was completely severed, surgery will not be able to repair that" he said. There was a severe comminuted fracture at the T10 vertebra with complete obliteration of the central canal from bony fragments. The vertebrae T7, T8 and T9 were fractured as well and several bony fragments were causing moderate to severe central canal stenosis at T7. I fractured every spinous process from the vertebrae C7 to T10, fractured ribs 6, 7, 8 and 11 on the left side, some of which being completely dislocated from the vertebral transverse processes. I had a C6-7 focal lordosis with central disk protrusion posteriorly, causing minimal canal stenosis. On the CT scan, a large paraspinous hematoma was seen ranging from the thoracolumbar junction up to T5. Minutes later in the MRI, it had expanded from the L2 vertebra all the way up to T4 and was displacing the heart and esophagus forward. I was also bleeding in my left lung. While my spinal cord was completely cut at T10 initially, which was what I found out by myself minutes after the accident, the other injuries had damaged the cord at the level of T7. The situation just kept getting worse. It was clear by then that the damage would not be reversible. With that new knowledge in mind, I was brought up to the Neuro Critical Care Unit where, to be freed from the pain, I hoped I would die.

A Precarious Situation

Death had never seemed sweeter. It would have offered an easy way out from the cruel circumstances in which I found myself. The physical pain was horrific, but the agony, the sadness in my mind was excruciating, unbearable. My life had been good, I had been good, and I was ready to go, wherever it was that I should go. I thought about my family and my friends and wanted to have the chance to tell them not to be sad, and explain that death was the right thing for me, as it would deliver me from the most unfathomable psychological anguish and physical suffering.

I woke up some time later, in my small critical care unit room. It was dark, and I was hooked up to machines and intravenous lines. Shirley and Fred Langeland were next to me. My future seemed uncertain, at best. Would I live through the night? Would I be able to complete medical school? Where would I live? What would happen to me? So many questions continued to run through my mind as I lay there, semi-conscious.

I also had glimpses of positive thoughts about my friends Holly McGowan and Stan Clawson. Both were living with paraplegia and both were enjoying productive and fulfilling lives. It was encouraging to think that if they were happy despite their paralysis, I would likely learn to be happy also.

My neck was in a stabilizing cervical collar and I dared not to move my arms by fear of making my condition worse. I only moved the fingers of my right hand to hold my visitors' hands. I had a few visitors that evening. Heidi, a neurology resident and Amy, a plastic surgery resident with whom I had developed friendships both came in to say hi. The news of my accident spread through the tight knit hospital community like wildfire. Jana and Bill Rees, Grandpa John Langeland, Fred and Shirley Langeland, David Renner, some of the most influential people in my life were by my side at some point or another during this life changing event, and it was comforting to have them there.

CHAPTER 10

NEURO INTENSIVE CARE

The morning after my accident, I was taken to the operating theater where Dr. Meic Schmidt, a talented and highly skilled German neurosurgeon, performed a posterior fixation of my spinal column with Herrington rods during an eight-hour surgery which left me with a long midline posterior incision. Right before the surgery, I was so drugged up that my mind was playing tricks on me and, as I hallucinated, I thought that my friends Dr. Nelson, a general surgeon, and Dr. Rockwell, a plastic surgeon, came to wish me well as I was being wheeled out of my neuro intensive care room. Over time I realized that these memories might have been completely manufactured by a brain on high doses of opioids. Two weeks later, I would undergo a second neurosurgical procedure to affix plates to the anterior portion of my vertebrae for further stabilization, leaving me, this time, with several incisions over the right lung, and a chest tube.

All I remember from the post-operative period is the pain I was in. Each sudden movement triggered insufferable, sharp pain in my back and left ribs. Only a couple of days following my surgery, as I was trying to recuperate on the neurology floor, physical and occupational therapists were sent in to work with me. I simply saw the work as torture. The occupational therapists told me that the earlier they moved me, the better my recovery would be. I didn't buy it. Of course I wanted to maximize my recovery, but my spinal cord was completely cut and there was no recovery that could realistically be hoped for. In the big spectrum of things, giving me an extra few days to recover after surgery wouldn't negatively impact my overall outcome. My back made popping sounds each time I was being manipulated, and each time, it felt as if my back was being shattered. The left sided rib pain was even sharper than the back pain. Soon, the occupational therapist I nicknamed "tornado" became the unwelcomed enemy. I knew that it was difficult for people to understand the level of pain I experienced, as I hardly understood it myself. Quickly, I adamantly refused therapies that triggered more pain than I could bear.

Amy Sanders asked me if I wanted her to call Brooks Rohlen who was living in San Francisco at the time while doing an intern year in surgery. I responded that I would be happy to see him. He showed up what seemed like the next day with his girlfriend Rachel Ward. They brought me a poster of the upcoming Squaw Valley Prom, a few Squaw Valley Freestyle Skiing hats and a black Predator ski jacket with patches of all the Charity Smith sponsors, that I proudly wore during a TV interview for the local news.

Essentially, I had been in an atrocious amount of pain from the moment I entered the hospital and the pain continued on as I spoke with the TV news reporter on March 8th, four days after the accident. I explained that in 31 years of being alive, I had never thought that pain could be this severe. In fact, I never imagined that anyone could endure so much pain without passing out. During the same video segment, Fred Langeland said that I was a very capable young man with a lot of potential and my new state of paralysis wouldn't change that.

My dear classmates put together a grooming committee where girls came to take care of my physical appearance. They had come to help me clean up prior to the television interview and various photo ops for local newspapers. They did my hair and shaved my face. I looked like a million dollars, sort of.

Initially, the nurses gave me sponge baths and, try as they might to gently rock me on my sides to wash my back, the motion provoked excruciating pain. On the fifth day after the accident, I was transported to the ward's shower room. First, a metallic frame was placed above me in bed. Then, a mesh attached to one side of the frame was rolled under me as I laid on one side. I was then rolled back over the mesh and onto my other side while the mesh was pulled from under me and attached to the other side of the frame. Straps were pulled on each side, tightening the hammock-looking contraption and lifting my body off the bed in the process. I had lines of pain running through my back where the straps were traveling the width of the mesh. I was then wheeled to the shower room across the hallway, where I would get showered while my body lay there, immobile on the mesh. This, I recall, was the most uncomfortable shower I ever took.

Interestingly, they used the same method to change the bed sheets while I lay in the bed, that is, by rolling me side to side and pulling the sheet from under me. I thought it to be quite an ingenious technique.

NEUROLOGY UNIT

It was while on the neurology floor that I met Dr. Jeffrey Rosenbluth, the spinal cord injury rehabilitation attending and Dr. Derek Krete, a Physical Medicine and Rehabilitation resident. They explained to me that I would be transferred to the rehab unit whenever I would be medically stable.

Because it had been a few days since my accident, I asked the nurses if I had had a bowel movement and they answered that I hadn't had one yet. Suddenly, I wondered how I would ever be able to have one.

While recuperating from the first surgery in room 311 on the neuro floor, I waxed and waned in and out of consciousness due to the high doses of opioids I was being given in order to manage the pain. Initially, I had so many visitors that I didn't really have time to grieve my loss. People were visiting me all day long which prevented me from engaging in deep reflection over what had happened to me, and, in retrospect, perhaps it was a good thing as too much reflection at a time of despair can be counter-productive. Each time I opened my eyes, seven new visitors were hovering around my bed, and each time, I felt as though it was my duty to somehow entertain them.

I tried to talk to people but the words coming out of my mouth differed from what I was trying to say. My imagination ran so wild that I could have effortlessly written a magnificent fairy tale of utter nonsense. Clearly, drugs were not agreeing with me.

At the time, I was continuously hooked up to a pulse oximeter to monitor the level of oxygenation in my blood. Because of my broken ribs, and the opioids which suppressed the breathing process, my oxygenation was frequently low, triggering the alarm. Consequently, at night, I would only sleep sporadically in between alarms. When I did sleep, I always had the same dream, a vision of me snowboarding in the expert park at Snowbird. Each time the alarm rang, I would fall and break my back all over again. This would happen, it seemed, about ten times a night and was dreadful. These experiences were clearly some variant of post-traumatic stress disorder. My night nurse was a very nice guy who spent a lot of time talking to me and comforting me after these fear-triggering episodes.

Because of the time difference, my brother David had not been notified of my accident until late Sunday March 5th. My friend Diane told me later that, as she thought I might not survive my first night, she didn't want to make one phone call on Saturday to explain that I was paralyzed, only to call back the next day to explain that I had not survived. Also, the anxiety surrounding the purpose of the call certainly had something to do with its delay. David explained that as he learned about my accident over the phone from Diane, she was sobbing so profusely that he wasn't really sure what had happened and thought that I had died. He was in shock. He then called Fred Langeland who calmly, methodically, professionally laid out the facts. David said it was the first time he had ever heard the term "severe spinal cord injury." He asked if I was expected to ever be able to walk again. The answer was a resounding: "No." He then had the difficult task of transmitting this information to our parents. Trying to highlight the positive, he explained to my mom that I had been in an accident and that fortunately, I underwent surgery to stabilize my back, and while I wouldn't be able to walk again, I was doing well and had retained the use of my arms. He then called my dad who responded with anger and complete denial.

David immediately took time off from work and jumped on the first available plane and landed in Salt Lake City on Wednesday March 8th. He was diligent in filtering the constant flow of visitors so that I wouldn't be exhausted all the time. He would come at 8:30am and would leave at dinner time only to come right back after dinner to stay with me until 10:00pm. Each morning, he would read me the emails that family members and friends had sent throughout the night and we would respond to them as a group.

Dr. Jacinda Sampson a neurology resident, brought two books for me to read, although I unfortunately couldn't keep my eyes opened long enough to read anything. Eventually over the ensuing year, I was able to read one of the books she had brought titled: "The Curious Incident of the Dog in the Night-Time" by British author Mark Haddon, which is an amazing book that I highly recommend, written from the perspective of a young boy with an autism spectrum condition. The other book was: "A Whole New Life: An Illness and a Healing" by Reynolds Price, in which Price, a James B. Duke Professor of English at Duke University recalls the events surrounding his sudden paralysis from a spinal cord tumor. Finally, my dear friend Angelia Murdock gifted me the all-powerful book: "Night" by Elie Wiesel, which is an absolute must-read account of his experience in the Nazi German concentration camps at Auschwitz and Buchenwald during the second world war. This inspiring book showed me that life-changing events can come in a variety of shapes and forms and can scar us emotionally and physically, but, as the nineteenth century German Philosopher Friedrich Nietzsche said: "That which does not kill us, makes us stronger." Through the reading of others' stories and struggles, I became acutely aware of the fact that my own health issues, no matter how unsurmountable they appeared at the time, were, in the big scheme of things, quite trivial, and that some people have to live through significantly more difficult situations than I will ever face, despite my paralysis.

CHAPTER 11

REHABILITATION PART 1: THE SETTING

It did not take very long before I was brought to the rehab floor where it was expected that I participate in both physical and occupational therapy sessions several times daily. I dreaded these sessions. The therapists were kind, but again, the pain I experienced made it impossible for me to do anything during the first few days. The expectations placed upon me were just too much to handle, at a time when all I needed was some alone time to deal with my new circumstances. At night, for physiological reasons that I did not comprehend, my upper body, above the lesion was sweating profusely. The bed sheets had to be changed from under me up to three times each night. The gowns I was sleeping in were so drenched, they had to be changed with equal frequency. A towel was placed on my pillow to absorb the sweat from my neck. It was uncomfortable to say the least, and I saw little improvement in the course of my hospitalization. I was prescribed Oxybutynin, an antimuscarinic therapy, in an attempt to reduce the sweating, but this drug had for sole effect to dry my mouth and my eyes bringing even more discomfort to my already troubled nights. Every two hours, an aid or a nurse would come in to turn me to prevent pressure sores, and I wondered if I would ever be able to do that at home. I was advised to set an alarm clock every two hours to turn, and to catheterize my bladder every four hours. I figured that I could sleep up to ten hours before my accident without having to go to the bathroom, and the fact that I was now paralyzed, should not change the ability of my bladder to hold on to urine for longer than four hours. Also, I thought that if I trained my bladder to be drained every four hours, thus not allowing the volume to reach beyond 400mL, then pretty soon, my bladder would shrink and not be able to stretch beyond that volume. Therefore, I made sure to let it reach 600mL quite frequently, initially, so that it remained flexible. I kept very detailed records of my urine output and realized that the output doubled at night which could be explained by the resorption of the fluid accumulated throughout the day in my distal legs from immobility.

I would ask to be awoken at 7am promptly at which time I needed to be given 15mg of Oxycodone, without which I simply was not able to initiate any movement at all due to pain. The pain was in my back, but even more so in my left thoracic cage. Before falling asleep, I always made arrangements for a male aide to come pick me up at 7:15am to carry me from the bed to the shower chair. I would then take a shower to rid myself of the night sweat and, to some degree, wash away the pain. I would then return to my room to eat breakfast, brush my teeth, and get back to bed to wait for my occupational therapist, Lindey, to come make me practice how to get dressed in bed in the supine or seated position. At first, I relied heavily on the side railings to get myself in the sitting position from which I was supposed to put on my socks and my pants, but little by little, I was able to sit up by grabbing onto the side of the bed with one hand while pushing on the mattress with the other. After the occupational therapy session, I usually had 30 minutes of rest before a physical therapy student would come get me. In physical therapy, I would practice transferring from the bed to the chair and to and from an elevated mat in the gym. I often used a sliding board to perform these transfers. I had two sessions of each occupational and physical therapy daily. Occupational therapy was my favorite as I felt that I was learning the skills that I would be using daily in my life to come. Lindey taught me bed mobility, how to get dressed, how to get in and out of the shower, essentially, how to perform all the activities of daily living that I would heavily rely upon.

While in rehab, I heard people say a lot of things in an effort to be encouraging, but that unfortunately meant nothing when faced with a completely severed cord. "He's so strong willed, he'll walk in no time." Statements like these were only setting me up for failure. If I don't walk again in no time, will it imply I have no will? Similarly, overly optimistic statements regarding my physical abilities or how well my life would unfold initially bothered me. Someone told me that God had chosen me to be paralyzed so that my life could be used as an example for others. People were just trying to be helpful and didn't really know what to say or how to say it.

I also had to deal with the influx of emails from well-meaning people who had read about miraculous recoveries on the internet. Someone forwarded an article saying that a surgeon in Portugal had been able to reconnect severed spinal cords. I learned that people can be very gullible when desperately trying to reach for straws and find solutions that don't exist yet.

Living with paraplegia, I am what is called wheelchair-bound, meaning that I rely on the use of a wheelchair for mobility. For some reasons I can't fully pinpoint, I don't especially like this term, but the fact remains that whenever someone sees me, they also see the wheelchair. I learned this basic truth early on while in the hospital, when a woman stopped me in the hallway and said: "Wow! You are very good looking, considering." I wasn't just plain good looking anymore, I was good looking, considering.

A few days after I had been transferred to the rehab unit, Dr. Rosenbluth, my physiatrist, told me that another patient with a similar injury would be joining us on the floor. His name was Gavin, he was 28-years-old and had become a person with paraplegia at T-9, following a snowboarding accident in Park City. We became good friends as we learned to deal with our new circumstances together and shared the same pain and worries about the new life we were forced to embark on. Gavin was from out of town and his mother, a nurse, had chosen to stay with him throughout his hospitalization. She was the source of great emotional support. About a week after Gavin arrived, another.patient joined our crew. His name was Nick and he was a 15-year-old teenager who had been injured while driving an ATV on the sand dunes in southern Utah. He had rolled the ATV in a sharp turn and had broken his back. He had lost consciousness and upon waking up, had used his cell phone to alert his family that he was in a ditch and couldn't get up. He was flown to the University of Utah Hospital to undergo surgery and stay in rehab with us.

Throughout my medical education, I had been insured through Intermountain Health Care (IHC) with a decent premium and an excellent coverage. However, before starting my last year in medical school, the University of Utah asked me to be insured through the student health insurance plan. Little did I know, at the time, that the plan would prove to be of limited value. For a monthly premium higher than the one I used to pay with IHC, my coverage dropped from 1 million dollars to fifty thousand dollars. Hardly the same thing. Of course, fifty thousand dollars amounted to nothing in comparison to the cost of my overall stay in the hospital. Fortunately, Medicaid Emergency tackled some of the cost of my care during the first couple of days in the hospital. My student insurance took a long time to cover their part of the cost. The hospital social worker omitted to seek funds from my secondary insurance, namely, the insurance from the US snowboarding association, and I was later asked to look into the availability of these funds myself. I would receive, on average, about 3-5 letters a week from the Utah state attorney general, trying to get me to cover the overwhelming cost of my hospital stay before the hospital even attempted to collect payment from my insurance company. By the end of my hospitalization, I accumulated a one-foot high pile of bills and two of those bills were for $81,000 and $77,000 respectively, and requested payment for services rendered within two weeks of receipt. It's not that I didn't want to pay, but given that I was a student, had no money, and was still hospitalized on the rehabilitation unit, trying to get my life back, the payments would surely be missed and more threatening letters from the state attorney would ensue. Overall, my healthcare bill rose to $350,000, $100,000 of which was covered by various insurances and the rest of the balance was made payable by me.

While I was in rehab, the Dean of Student Affairs for the School of Medicine came to see me to tell me that I could drop out of medical school and they would try to refund my tuition for the semester. Of course, I declined. Dr. Babitz, who was in charge of overseeing the month of personal research we had to perform as seniors in medical school, kindly adapted the requirements of the month, to enable me to fulfill them from my hospital room. Ironically enough, the title of my research project which had been selected prior to my accident was: Prevention of common snowboarding injuries. I was also scheduled to take an ethics class for which attendance was mandatory. Obviously, due to the rigorous physical and occupational therapy schedule, I was not able to attend. As a compensatory measure, I was asked to write a 5-page essay for each day that I missed, for a total of 11 days. Writing these essays involved some research, and often, I would start writing after dinner and stay up until 4am in order to complete the assignments. Needless to say, I wasn't exactly fresh for my next day of therapies, but I was given no other option and had to do what had to be done.

The showers were interesting. The shower chair was brought close to the wall, at the perfect distance for me to be able to handle the knobs and the shower head without risking falling forward. If the water was cold as it hit my legs, my legs would respond by jumping in rapid sequence as if they came to life. My legs did not like the cold water and they attempted to move out of the way. Once, the spasms triggered were such that I ended up standing in front of my shower chair, on the wet tile. This was a rather scary experience. I could have gone straight down on my face and caused much more damage to my already hurting body. Thankfully, I grabbed the bars and by some miracle, managed to fall back down onto the chair.

Fred had brought me a shower gel to use, one I had never used before, and consequently, its scent was a novelty. This new scent strangely became a leitmotiv of this peculiar period of my life. Over the ensuing year, every now and again, I purchased the same shower gel and each time I smelled the scent, vivid images of my time in the hospital rushed to my mind. The scent was a reminder of the progress I had made since that time but eventually I decided I didn't need to be reminded anymore and switched product.

The showers seemed to help rid my body of the pain. Each day, I knew that the first 15 minutes leading to the shower would be the most painful, but the pain would improve by the time I came back from the shower. At the end of the shower, I pulled on a string to alert the aids and nurses that I was ready to come out. They would bring me three large warm towels. One for my head, one for my arms, torso and back, and one for my legs. I wrapped myself as best as I could for the way back to the room. There, I was pushed in front of the sink near my bed. The sink was a pedestal sink that extended away from the wall allowing for a wheelchair to roll underneath. Using it, I fell in love with accessible designs. I would put the brakes on and rest my elbows on the front part of the sink and it all felt very comfortable. Right behind the sink was a tall mirror that was slightly slanted down to enable people in wheelchairs to see themselves better. I had never given much thought to the importance of the positioning of mirrors in bathrooms, but when a mirror is positioned too high, wheelchair users can usually only see the top of their heads.

I enjoyed grooming myself in the morning because it gave me dignity. I wheeled myself to the sink in my room to complete the morning routine. I brushed my teeth, shaved, put some gel in my hair, applied deodorant and cologne, and finally, I was ready to start the day with a sense of normalcy.

It was recommended that once I went home, I shower at night and keep my clothes on the bed to enable me to get ready promptly in the morning. That idea didn't work for me. I like to shower in the morning. I would never consider leaving the house without having showered first. Also, I was sweating at night, so getting dressed straight from bed was definitely not an option for me. I would have to wake up, get in my chair, cruise to the shower, come back, and get dressed in bed. The process involved a few additional steps in the morning, but these were necessary steps as far as I was concerned.

CHAPTER 12

REHABILITATION PART 2:

THE SUPPORT

During the time I spent in the hospital, I received a lot of get-well cards and supportive letters from friends as well as from people I had never met before. I kept them all in a paper bag and read them from time to time when I get depressed as the feeling of gratefulness that reading them triggers helps me get over the hump.

My good friend Holly McGowan from Truckee, California, was one such friend who provided a great deal of support. She had become paraplegic 10 years prior from a motor vehicle accident. She was the only real friend I had in the wheelchair community before getting paralyzed myself. She wrote me encouraging letters and also sent me comfortable clothes to use while in therapies. Sweatpants, t-shirts of all colors, athletic shoes and slippers, she sent it all. Somehow, and I never knew it was possible, she had a huge case of fresh fruits sent to me from out of state. She also brought me cans of Cassoulet which she had picked up during a recent trip to France.

My friend Sergio Gonzales from medical school would visit me occasionally to get me the most professional haircuts I have ever had. His attention to detail was bewildering.

Gaby Vargas, another medical school friend was by my side daily. We had spent our first year of medical school sitting next to each other and had gone snowboarding together on a few occasions but when I got hurt, she took ownership of my well-being. It was comforting to be able to count on her presence by my side on a consistent basis. Even after I was discharged, she would visit me as often as she could and gave me rides anywhere I needed to go. Her dedication was very touching.

Another friend from medical school was visiting me daily, his name was Chris Dunkerley. He and his wife would come to have dinner with me and ask how my day had been. Trying to look upbeat for the sake of my visitors was challenging given that, deep down, I was mortified by fear and anxiety.

Dr. Elizabeth Allen, Associate Dean of Student Affairs and Education for the School of Medicine for my first three years in medical school gave me some advice that resonated so much with me that I frequently pass it on to my patients. She said, and I may paraphrase here, that it is all too easy to get overwhelmed when thinking about the future while trying to heal from an illness or an accident or simply while going through life. Instead, she said, just focus on today, focus on doing the best that you can, today, and leave the worrying for tomorrow, and of course, she pointed out, when tomorrow comes, it becomes today and thus, you never worry and continue to give your best while trying to keep your head up, day after day. What a marvelous piece of advice!

I also made new friends from out of the blue. One medical student from one of the classes below me and whom I had never met before brought me several DVDs he had rented out at Blockbuster so I could watch movies in the evening. People were kind and full of good intentions and it was humbling to be the recipient of so much love and care.

My college friend Ben Romney was attending medical school at Tufts University in Boston at the time of my accident. When he was notified of what had happened, he asked his older brother, Josh Romney, to come visit me on his behalf. Ben's email to me stated that Josh was a very generous man who would help me the same way he would have if he lived nearby. He wasn't kidding. I had met Josh on maybe two or three occasions while spending the weekend at their cabin in Deer Valley while Ben and I were in school together at Brigham Young University. But suddenly, Josh appeared in my hospital room, also with a bag full of DVDs, and told me that he had heard about my accident and was available to help in any way he could, all I had to do was ask. I was truly amazed by his candor. He and his wife Jen visited me often bringing outside food from Cafe Rio. While in the hospital I suffered a complete lack of appetite and frequent nauseous episodes and had chosen to limit my intake to plates of watermelons, pineapples and strawberries, but when Cafe Rio was brought in, my appetite returned!

As it was evident that I would not be able to return to live with Fred and Shirley given the ubiquity of stairs in the house, Josh said that he and Jen would be happy to have me come live with them. On the spot, he drew the floor map of the ground floor in his house and said that it would be perfect for the wheelchair. I can't imagine that it was thrilling to get a newly paralyzed person, one you barely know, into your home, into your life, when you are trying to start a family, yet, Josh and Jen made it sound exciting. They obviously must have had their doubts and concerns about the situation but they never let it show in front of me. I needed to be discharged somewhere after my inpatient rehab stay, and they would be there to catch me. They didn't make a big deal about it, they just said I was coming home with them, end of story. I get teary-eyed whenever I ponder the sacrifice they made by taking me into their lives. Promptly, Josh had a ramp built in his backyard to enable me to get into the house. They purchased a brand-new mattress for me to use because they knew I needed a soft bed to avoid pressure sores and Josh picked up my chair one day after therapy to make sure the doorways were wide enough and the chair could go throughout the house without problems.

AN ALLERGIC REACTION

Toward the end of my rehab stay I developed a weird allergic reaction that caused my skin to have raised blotches throughout, and my fingers swelled up like inflated latex gloves, to the point where I could no longer bend them. I was sent to the dermatology clinic but no one could put a finger on the culprit and it was thought that perhaps a prophylactic antibiotic used during my second surgery could be blamed for my reaction. I was treated with prednisone which had the side effect of throwing me into one of the deepest depressive episodes I have ever experienced. I remember lying in bed with my eyes closed, wanting to die. I refused to eat anything and when friends would drop by to visit, I would remain still with my eyes closed pretending to be asleep. The resident taking care of me explained that an IV would have to be placed if I didn't start eating but I couldn't care less. I wanted to slowly slide into oblivion. On the second day, Dr. Tomb, my Psychiatry Professor from medical school and a good friend of mine came into my room with a copy of an article explaining that sometimes, steroids throw people into dark depressions. Knowing the cause of my sudden despair helped me resurface. We tapered the steroids down and slowly, I tried to come back to my normal self. It was a struggle that lasted many days. On one of those days, I called Josh on his cell phone and crying, all I could say was: "Come get me, I'm sad, please come get me." And he did. He had planned to spend the afternoon with two of his friends, one of whom had come from out of town. They had rented a car and were looking forward to go race it on the Millersport racetrack. Now, all of a sudden, the rented car was parked still in the rehab parking lot and Josh was carrying me out. It was one of the most touching moments I have ever experienced and a turning point in my recovery. I wasn't alone and I had a friend who took me under his wing without thinking twice about it. He had sacrificed his afternoon of fun to come get me when I needed him. His friends came with him to get me and we figured out, for the first time, how to take down the wheelchair and store it in the trunk of the car. Josh asked me what I wanted to do and I said I just wanted to go home, where I used to live with Fred and Shirley. When we arrived at the house, Josh's friend carried me up the flight of stairs while Josh carried my wheelchair. I told the boys to go hang out for an hour or so and come back to get me later and I went into my room, by myself, for the first time since my accident.

The sheets had been stripped from the bed, the bedroom had been tidied up a bit, but the desk where my computer stood, all my papers and my books laid where they were some six weeks prior, the morning I had left for the snowboarding competition. It was as if time had stood still while I was experiencing the most challenging experience of my life. I transferred from the wheelchair onto the mattress and laid on my back. I looked at the window, the ceiling, the closet, the desk. I looked around this familiar room and realized that nothing had changed, everything was the same. Everything was the same, or almost. My baby rabbits had been moved to a different house where my medical school friend Chris Dodgion was kindly caring for them. Now, a wheelchair was by the bed, standing as a reminder of my newly acquired paralysis, as a reminder that my life had been forever altered, that things, never, would be the same. I really wasn't there to stay. I wasn't taking an afternoon nap in my bedroom. I couldn't walk down the stairs by myself as I had done thousands of times. I was just there to visit, briefly, before being carried back to my hospital bed. I laid there in silence, I closed my eyes, and I cried.

CHAPTER 13
HOSPITAL DISCHARGE

I was discharged from the hospital on May 2nd, 2006, nearly two months after having been brought in by helicopter. Chris Dunkerley had insisted on being the one picking me up to bring me to Jen and Josh's house. Upon leaving the rehabilitation unit I was given a long list of medications I was supposed to continue taking. While I had been completely oblivious to the fact that I would be asked to continue taking certain medications, I was even more naïve with regard to their cost. Chris however, had anticipated that the pharmacy bill would be hefty and had brought $400 in cash to give to me, to cover a one-month supply of medications no longer covered by insurance since my insurance coverage had plateaued. The $400 didn't even cover the cost. I asked the pharmacist to hand back the list so I could make some alterations and remove the medications I didn't think were absolutely necessary. I was so fortunate to have a charitable trust account set up on my behalf at Zions Bank because it helped me pay for all the medications I would be needing to cover on my own for the ensuing few months until the new year started and the insurance coverage was reset. One particular medication stands out in my mind: It is the antibiotic Levofloxacin which was prescribed to me for urinary tract infections that I frequently suffered due to the need for self-catheterization as a mean of emptying my bladder. The cost of the Levofloxacin course, at the time, was $127. That personal experience with the cost of medications made me passionate to learn more on the topic of pharmacoeconomics and I always keep in mind the cost of therapies when writing prescriptions for patients.

I moved in with Jen and Josh Romney who had a ramp built so that I could access the main floor of their beautiful home. The very first week-end after my discharge from the hospital, before I could get accustomed to life outside a controlled environment like the hospital used to be, I had to board a plane and travel to Los Angeles to sit for the USMLE Step 2-CS examination, the last official clinical skills examination during medical school. My friend Matt McIff's father, Mark McIff, a Judge from Southern Utah had offered, as an act of kindness, to pay for my trip to L.A. It was my first time on a plane as a person with paraplegia. We had gotten a hotel room and went to eat at Sizzler across the street the night before the examination. While at Sizzler, we saw a rambunctious group of French tourists. When they left, they walked right through the back door which read: "Do not open, alarm will ring." Once back at the hotel, at the front desk, while the receptionist was already assisting another guest, a French woman came barging to the desk, almost pushing aside the guest already being helped and asked, in French, where her room was located. I was reminded of the culture I had come from where public order is an afterthought. I also realized that I had been in the United States a long time and was more comfortable with American customs than I was with French ones, and the behavior of the French tourists appeared as foreign to me, as it did to Matt or any other American.

Upon returning to Salt Lake City, I spent two weeks in a class where medical students were encouraged to write poetry about their experiences in medical school. I really enjoyed this opportunity to reflect, not only on my experience as a care provider, but also, on my experience as a patient.

The new Associate Dean of Students Affairs and Education at the School of Medicine, Dr. Barbara Cahill, a genuinely kind person who provided me with a lot of encouragement and support, worked very hard to set up a schedule that would allow me to graduate from medical school with a minimum amount of delay.

In May 2006, my medical school class was graduating, and, despite the postponement caused by my hospitalization, I was allowed to participate in the graduation ceremony with my classmates. Just shy of 4 years since the white coat ceremony, we were back at Kingsbury Hall to receive our Medical Degree, or in my case, a paper telling me that my Medical Degree would be mailed to me once I had successfully completed my last two rotations. We wore the traditional Doctoral robes and Gaby had helped me get mine since I had been in the hospital during the ordering process. It was quite a momentous occasion, only made better, and more emotional, by an unforeseen twist. My name beginning with a Y, again, I was placed toward the end of the line. When my name was called, as I proceeded to push myself forward to enter the stage, everybody in the auditorium stood up to give me a standing ovation. I was overwhelmed and stopped to look around and take in the experience. It was an unforgettable moment. I had the urge to bow back as a sign of respect and propped myself up by pushing on the wheelchair's armrests and bowed my head in humility before continuing to propel the chair across the stage to shake hands with Dr. David Bjorkman, Dean of the School of Medicine.

CHAPTER 14

THE POWER OF DREAMS

At Josh and Jen's house, I would stay up very late at night, watching the network TLC and, in particular, a show called "Shalom in the Home" hosted by Rabbi Shumley Boteach. He had a soft way of counseling people about issues in their lives. I stayed up late because I was afraid of the night. I was afraid of being incontinent, and I was afraid of not falling asleep fast enough and being left staring at the ceiling with thoughts of despair. I was also afraid of the morning.

I woke up every morning in a state of great sadness. I woke up to the realization that I couldn't walk. One might think that I would understand quickly that I could no longer walk, but even months after the injury, I would wake up and realize that I was paralyzed, all over again. The reason why I instantly thought I could walk in the seconds upon awakening was because my dreams had convinced me that I could.

While in the hospital, my dreams were nothing but nightmares and I continuously relived my crash and helicopter ride. Once I was discharged from the hospital, my dreams became more optimistic. It was the month of

May, spring was in full swing, the weather was gorgeous and my legs would be no exception to the generalized rebirth that takes place in the springtime. Surely, they would start working again, or so my unconscious thoughts seemed to believe as evidenced by the dreams I was having at the time.

I used to have superpowers in my dreams and was able to fly or at least float if I focused on it intently. There was no flying around this time. I dreamed that I was in a wheelchair. I remember a few of these dreams very clearly.

One took place in a city I did not recognize. The neighborhood where I found myself was on a hillside. The night had already fallen and it was dark outside. All my dreams took place at night like in an episode of Scooby Doo. A few weak yellow street lamps were trying as best they could to brighten the area. I was in a wheelchair, pushing myself to a booth on the side of the road that looked like one you would find at a flea market. It was located on the up side of a horizontal, leveled street, near the intersection with a perpendicular street, itself going up and down. Someone had laid out many pieces of equipment relating to wheelchairs. Old brakes, wheels, casters, screws, and axles. The person tending the booth told me this was a place where other wheelchair users would come to trade wheelchair parts and that many were on their way there. I waited. People eventually came and either traded or bought the equipment they needed for their wheelchairs as I looked on. Suddenly, I recognized a familiar face in the crowd and I stood up from my chair to go greet my friend. My wheelchair then proceeded to roll down the vertical street. I ran after it. The street ended a couple of blocks later right before a river which was running at the bottom of the hill. The wheelchair disappeared in the water. Some stairs were going down toward the river where my wheelchair had fallen. I stood at the top of the stairs wondering whether I should bother getting wet to retrieve this wheelchair that I obviously no longer needed for some miraculous reasons, as after all, I had been able to stand to greet my friend, and run after the chair while it rolled out of control down the hill and into the river. I immediately woke up, happy to be cured. I opened my eyes, and with all the joy in the world, believing as hard as I could that the dream had foreseen my miraculous healing, I tried to swing my legs out of bed only to realize that I couldn't. The lack of spontaneous movement in my legs instantaneously brought me back to the sad reality; I was still paralyzed. And so, morning after morning, I was faced with the tragic reality that I was paralyzed, and had to deal with it emotionally, as if for the first time, all over again.

My early dreams continued, with me being in a wheelchair initially, and on occasion, out of the blue, I could stand up and walk away from it, only to wake up heartbroken. As time passed, it was harder and harder for me to walk out of the chair. Progressively, my gait worsened. I would walk hunched over like a very old man. It was difficult for me to keep my head up because of the severe kyphosis that had developed in my back. I could walk still, but not very well, very fast or very far.

Another dream that I recall clearly, marked another landmark. I managed to shuffle forward despite the worsening curvature in my back, but I felt, with great sadness, that my walking days were coming to an end. I hobbled my way to a friend's front door and called out his name while circling his lawn. When he came out, I explained that I dared not to stop moving as I was afraid I wouldn't be able to start walking again if I stopped. I asked if he could walk with me to keep me from falling asleep, to keep me from losing the use of my legs. I don't remember the rest of the dream. I must have grown tired and stopped walking. When I woke up the next morning, I knew I was paralyzed and would never walk again.

    I spent the following dreams in a wheelchair and was no longer able to walk, until two years later. The dream took place at the Bellagio in Las Vegas. I came in with my mother and after trying to push the wheelchair over the ultra-thick carpet of the casino floor, I decided to check my wheelchair in at the coat closet and to walk instead which had become unusual at that time. The interesting part came at the end of the dream. When it came time to leave the hotel, as we were waiting for a taxi in the atrium, I exclaimed that I had almost forgotten my wheelchair and told my mother how terrible this would have been to leave it behind. I could not afford to be separated from my wheelchair, it was a part of me and I needed it to go on. It was with great relief that I was reunited with my wheelchair. As I woke up, I was reassured to see it waiting for me at the bedside. I pondered the meaning of this dream. I was able to store my wheelchair somewhere when it was not the most convenient for me to use and was able to walk without any difficulties whatsoever. Eventually, I came back to the wheelchair on my own with relief for not having lost it. I suppose I came to terms with what an intricate part of my life the wheelchair had become and how very necessary it was for me never to be separated from it in real life, but that I could also do without it, in my dreams. I was not sad to see it waiting for me at the side of the bed, I was happy it was there, I was relieved. I have not used a wheelchair in my dreams since that time, and, in the darkness of the night, I walk again.

CHAPTER 15

RETURN TO INDEPENDENT LIVING PART 1:

GETTING AROUND

After about a month of living with Jen and Josh, a new apartment building opened at the corner of 400 South and 300 East in Salt Lake City, right behind my favorite Mexican restaurant Su Casa, and Josh took me there to look at handicap accessible apartments. I selected one on the 6th floor. Mark and Ann Marie Pace, my uncle and aunt from the Langeland family were upgrading all the furniture in their home, and enough pieces were brought over to entirely furnish my new living quarters. My rabbits Calypso and Edonis were brought back to me. Fred and Shirley took me to the store to purchase everything someone needs in a home and just like that, I was set! Or almost. I still needed a vehicle to get around. As I pondered what vehicle would best meet my needs, I reflected on the various modes of transport I had had since moving to the United States.

In 1995, I had gone to REI to purchase a $300 mountain bike which I used to go to school while attending the Salt Lake Community College. Two years later, I took a $3,100 loan from Zions First National Bank, co-signed by Fred, of course, as no bank would lend me any money given that I was not a US Citizen and had no job, and bought a mighty red 1992 Geo Metro which would later affectionately be known, as "the blood clot." My car payments were $115 a month. It was a small car with a small engine. Let me rephrase this, it was a very small car with a very small engine. A 3-cylinder, 1 Liter engine in fact. It wasn't much, but it was mine and I took great care of it. Well, sort of. I had no mechanical background whatsoever and didn't have a single clue about what was going on under the hood. What I did know however, was how to detail a car and make it look spiffy. While my car was modest in appearance, it always looked spotless, all the way until the day I heard a big "claketyclak" from the engine compartment after turning on the engine. I took it to a mechanic who proposed to charge me $70 to "run some tests" to see what the problem could be. I declined his most generous offer and instead opted to call my brother David in France so he could listen to the engine and diagnose the problem over the phone. To me, it sounded like somebody was beating a wrench inside of the engine block. To him, it sounded like one of the piston rods had snapped. Something told me he was right. While I was busy deep cleaning the exterior of my car, I had forgotten to change the oil every 3,000 miles. I had done it, just not frequently enough, obviously, as demonstrated by my car's demise. I kept driving it, on 2 cylinders, between December 1997 and April 1998. As I was stopped at a red light going northbound on 1300 East just south of 500 South, the usual "clakety" sound made a final loud "KLUNG" and the engine abruptly stopped.

A nice guy who was in the car behind me helped me push the Geo to the side of the road and was kind enough to give me a ride home. During the short ride he asked me why I was in the US and I explained that I was a student at the Salt Lake Community College and wanted to go to medical school. He said that once I would be a doctor, I would be able to buy a new car, and wished me luck.

I left for France in June 1998 to go fulfill my duties in the French Military and left the car parked in John Langeland's covered parking. Upon returning to Salt Lake City in December 1999, I took the car to a shop to get the defunct engine replaced with a rebuilt engine. $1,200 later, the blood clot was back on the road full swing. It handled the round-trips from Provo to Salt Lake City every weekend while I was attending Brigham Young University and never left me stranded by the side of the road again. It was a trustworthy little machine. Of course, it had some issues as one would expect in a car that inexpensive. The handle supposed to activate the windshield wipers was missing since the day I had purchased the car making it unusable in the rain or snow. I had mentioned it to my friend Xavier Gache over dinner while in France. His dad, Alain, after hearing my lack of fortune, left the dinner table and returned a few minutes later with a small chrome metal stick, the length of a toothbrush, about 5mm in diameter with a knob on one end. He explained that it was an old lever used to trigger the flushing mechanism of a toilet and that I should try sticking it in the dashboard to use as the windshield wiper handle. I brought my precious flush handle all the way back to the US, and to my greatest surprise, it fit in the hole in the dashboard wonderfully, forever enabling me to make use of the windshield wipers. As time went on, other problems crept up, notably, the driver's window. It was a manual window but somehow the mechanism inside the door panel had gotten warped and the window could no longer go up or down. I soon learned that it was against the law, at least in Utah, to not be able to lower the window, when the car was rejected at the annual state safety inspection. I couldn't afford to get it fixed and Shirley generously offered to pay the repair cost so that I could pass the inspection. The repair was short lived, unfortunately, and the window remained mostly unusable making the 47-mile commute to Provo, in the summer, without air conditioning, quite uncomfortable. Eventually, the keyhole gave out on the driver's door and if I wanted the car to be locked, I had to lock it from the inside and exit from the passenger side after gracefully wrestling my way from seat to seat in the small cabin in a way that would make an Olympic gymnast proud. Soon enough, I got tired of the gymnastic workout, exited the car from the driver's side and left the car unlocked. No one in their right mind would steal it anyway. One day in the summer, I walked to my car and noticed that the driver door was pink while the rest of the car was red. Little by little the color had fainted, and in the morning sun, the color change became obvious. The car had likely been in an accident in the past and the door had been repainted. In December 2001, running out of money on my student loans, I could no longer afford the car insurance or the maintenance. The rebuilt engine was working well, but everything else was falling apart. I decided to give the car away to a married couple from Haiti who was living in Provo at the time. They were more destitute than I was, and perhaps they could use the car to commute to and from a job.

In the spring of 2002, having been accepted to medical school at the University of Utah, I knew I had to acquire a new means of transportation. A car was too expensive, so I opted to get a scooter instead. I had gone to the Yamaha dealership to "look around" and fell in love with the silver and chrome vino scooter. It was a 50cc engine with sluggish acceleration, a concept I was very familiar with. Even though I had no job and no money, the salesman authorized a loan with the Yamaha credit department for the $1,900 purchase and the payments were set at $30 a month for what appeared to be the rest of my life. I bought a shiny silver helmet and took the beast on the road. Driving in the evening in the summer, I felt like a giant bug magnet. The bugs were attracted by the headlight and dove with great enthusiasm in my eyes, my hair and my mouth, so I decided to mount a windshield on the vino, adding yet a little more flair to this already stunning machine.

The best part about the vino was the convenient parking. During the first two years of medical school, I parked under the pharmacy building about 300 ft from the door of the Browning auditorium where lectures were held. During the last two years of medical school, while on clinical rotations, whether assigned to LDS hospital, the VA or the University Hospital, I could always park the vino within 300ft of the entrance when others had a rough time finding parking for their cars. There were, alas, some inconveniences as well. From early November until the end of February the cold was biting. I wore a wool scarf around my neck, chin and mouth, a snow hat under the helmet, leather gloves, and despite wrapping myself like a burrito on Cinco de Mayo before going out, the cold quickly penetrated the multiple layers of clothing. The wind factor to consider when riding at 30 miles an hour in an open vehicle only aggravated the cold. The farthest I could travel, I decided, was 20 city blocks, the distance from Fred and Shirley's house to Sugarhouse where I tried to go once a week to catch a movie at the dollar theater. One block more and I would surely freeze to death. I somehow managed to get around with the vino in the snow for four consecutive winters and only fell once while driving on an icy road. Fortunately, I only suffered minor scratches. In four years of faithful service, I drove the vino over 10,000 miles and it never broke down.

Between my second and third year in medical school, I saw a white 1985 Chevy Blazer on a parking lot in the student village with a price tag of $1,300. I thought it would be nice to get a car again, to enable me to go to the mountain on week-ends, so I called the number on the window sign. The owner showed me the Blazer. It had a new muffler and new tires and was a 4x4 which I really liked. He asked me if I intended to drive far with it and I said that I would just go back and forth to big cottonwood canyon. He said that it was preferable not to drive too far because the seats were uncomfortable. I soon figured out the reason for not wanting to drive too far had nothing to do with the seats being uncomfortable. I negotiated the price down to $1,100 and gave the owner a check against which he gave me the title of the vehicle with a letter stating that I bought the car "as is." It overall appeared to be a very functional vehicle for me.

The following week-end, I drove down to Provo to show my newly purchased all-terrain vehicle to my friend Yann. I was about 20 miles from Provo when I heard the loud and familiar "clakety" sound. I kept driving and barely made it to Provo. As I entered the parking lot of the condominium building, Yann was waiting for me. The "clakety" noise was louder than ever and green fluid was being dumped onto the asphalt. What a sweet Blazer I had just bought! I got one week out of it before it imploded. I obviously had to leave it in Provo and Yann got it towed to an engine shop the next day where the engine would be replaced with a rebuilt engine. The price tag was $2,500, more than twice the price of the vehicle itself.

Thirteen months after replacing the engine with a one-year warranty, as I was coming back to Salt Lake City on Interstate 15 from a dinner at Yann's house on a Sunday afternoon, the Blazer died again. The work was now out of warranty and the repairs amounted to $1,250, which money I didn't have, but Fred offered to help with the cost and the engine was replaced, for the second time. Two weeks after I took the blazer out of the shop again, I drove to Snowbird for the snowboarding competition from which I came back aboard a helicopter.

Along with losing the ability to walk, I lost the ability to drive a car with a manual gear box. I was told that I could only drive an automatic vehicle using hand controls. The Blazer, of course had a manual gear box. After all the money invested in making it quasi functional from a mechanical standpoint, I was unable to drive it. My friend Gaby Vargas had helped me tremendously throughout my hospitalization and she mentioned that her sister, brother in law and their children were moving to Utah from El Salvador and that they came with nothing. I decided to give them the newly repaired blazer. It would be a good car for them.

I then found myself not only paralyzed, but without any vehicle to get around after my discharge from the hospital. During my two-month hospitalization, one of my many tasks was to find a suitable vehicle.

Amid the constant depressive state I was in while in the hospital, browsing the internet in search of the car that would best fit my new needs as a person with paraplegia, was always, reliably, the highlight of my day.

My physical therapist, Sue Sandwick, made it clear that I needed a car low to the ground to avoid putting too much strain on my shoulders during the transfer from the wheelchair to the car and vice versa. I had a few requirements of my own. First, I was hoping to get a reliable car. One that wouldn't leave me stranded on I-15 coming back from a Sunday dinner with my friends from Provo. I had experienced it and had no intention of re-living the experience, albeit, with the added bonus of being seated in a wheelchair on the side of the road. The second requirement I was hoping to fulfill was to acquire an all-wheel drive vehicle to decrease the chances of getting stuck somewhere in the snow in the winter months. A single problem stood strong between my wish to get a new car and its actual purchase: Money. I didn't have any. By the time I was transferred from the ICU to the rehabilitation unit, I learned that some of my medical school friends took the initiative to start a relief fund on my behalf. The account was created at Zions Bank and was called: Gael Yonnet Special Needs Trust and Shirley Langeland became the Trustee.

CHAPTER 16

FUNDRAISING EFFORTS

The purpose of the special needs account was to help me buy the adaptive equipment that would enable me to live as normal a life as possible. My friends managed to gather donations from a large number of local businesses and had set up a raffle where people could buy tickets to win a chance to take home those kindly donated items. They had set up a booth in the hospital hallway and asked passersby if they were interested in purchasing raffle tickets. Other friends created fundraisers on their own.

Larry Daugherty was a medical student in the class below me and was a registered instructor for Basic and Advanced Life Support classes from the American Heart Association. People paid him to teach them as well as test and certify their knowledge. He dedicated a few classes to my cause and donated all the money he had earned to my special needs trust. Brooks Rohlen, founder and chairman of the Charity Smith Foundation created a special scholarship to help raise money for the trust. Dr. Ingebretsen, head of the Wilderness Medicine class also donated money. Dr. David Renner my mentor throughout medical school and his partner Brian Rivette insisted on buying my first wheelchair.

When KSL, the local TV station aired a news segment about my accident in the evening news, they mentioned that money could be donated into the trust and two newspaper articles also made mention of that fact. Consequently, a plethora of people whom I had never met in my life deposited money directly into the Zions Bank account. The support I received from the community was positively overwhelming. I felt strengthened to know that so many people cared about me and were willing to sacrifice their hard-earned money to help me get the best chance of recovering the most functional life possible.

I truly believe that the only reason why I am still alive today despite the tremendous despair I have at times endured is because of the support of all these people. I couldn't let the darkness win. I owe it to all those who sacrificed on my behalf to live the fullest and happiest life possible. When one comes to think of it, I was given so much that there is really no excuse for me not to be fulfilled and happy.

. My friend Charlie Huebner from Strong Audi in Salt Lake City had earned my trust when he allowed me to drive vehicles during my medical school years although I would come to the dealership on a scooter. Naturally, we contacted each other while I was in the hospital and he helped me find the perfect car, heavily discounted, and arranged for hand controls to be installed, courtesy of Audi. Having no job, I couldn't qualify for a regular loan and Brian Rivette loaned me the money necessary to purchase a used Audi A4 quattro with only 11,000 miles. The charitable donations as well as a sizeable gift from my mother in France who had just inherited a little bit of money, enabled me to repay the loan quickly. I was in love with this car! It was the best car I could have dreamed of and it met my needs perfectly.

During my two months in the hospital, no one showed me how to get in and out of a car. When I went to pick up my car at Strong Audi with David Renner and Brian Rivette, I had to figure out on the spot how to get myself in, and how to get the chair in also. It presented a bit of a challenge. It was obvious that the car could be damaged in the process if I wasn't careful. It took me what seemed like 30 minutes to get in and out the first time. Later, with more practice, more strength, and after having developed my own technique, I was able to get in or out of my car in less than a minute. I figured a way where, after putting my right leg in the car and throwing myself head first on the driver seat, I would take off the cushion and place it upside down on the passenger seat. Then, I would remove the side protectors and put them on the cushion. After that, I would pop off the first wheel adjacent to the car and place it on the floor behind the passenger seat. Then, I would turn the chair over to remove the other wheel and place it onto the back seat. That is where the beauty of the anti-tippers came into play. They allowed the chair to stay upright without the wheels. Otherwise, the chair would flip and hit the car. After removing the anti-tippers and resting the chair on the door frame, I had to lift the chair into the car. Bringing the chair in the car is easier said than done, and that was the tricky part to figure out. I did it by counterbalancing the weight of the chair by gripping the opening for the sunroof with my right hand, while lifting the chair with the left hand. To accomplish this feat, the left hand had to be placed precisely at the center of gravity under the chair to keep it balanced. Then, I brought the chair over my chest, at which point the right hand replaced the left under the chair, and the left hand gripped the upper door frame while I lowered the chair over the passenger seat with the front casters facing forward. I repeated this sequence in reverse to get out of the car. After having learned the technique, I went to the hospital to show another spinal cord patient, Randy, how to get it done to prevent him from having to figure it all out on his own. I was now part of a community of people living with disabilities and the act of sharing this type of information that could facilitate one's life seemed essential.

CHAPTER 17

RETURN TO INDEPENDENT LIVING PART 2: A PAINFUL TRANSITION

While the struggle with pain management continued for a few months after my hospital discharge, it obviously took its roots early in my hospitalization.

In the first part of my hospitalization, after the second surgery, I had been on a PCA (Patient Controlled Analgesic) pump. This is a device where the patient has semi-control over the amount of pain medication he or she is receiving by pushing on a button when he or she needs another dose. A maximum dose per unit of time is set by the physician and the patient self-administers the pain medications as he or she sees fit within these parameters. As I was laying there with a chest tube on my right side in some of the most acute pain I had ever experienced, I was pushing the trigger as frequently as I could between dozing episodes, aware that only so much medication could be given every five minutes, but afraid to miss getting the maximum allotted dose to control my raging pain. Josh

Romney later told me that I pushed the button every few seconds.

The opioids made me loopy and made me speak a lot of nonsense. It also made me hallucinate and confabulate. One afternoon, a visiting friend asked me how I was doing, and I promptly answered, as truthfully as I could: "This afternoon, a few friends and I took a very small travel trailer and we all went to the beach in southern France to go surfing." I remember clearly speaking these words because they described the only images that came to my mind and while I was aware that these events hadn't happened, I couldn't come up with anything else to say. This particular instance, I recall following the statement with: "Do you remember what I said about going to the beach in a trailer? I made it up, I don't think it really happened." I was aware that the words coming out of my mouth didn't make sense, and was quite worried and embarrassed about it.

Pain remains elusive for most physicians who do not know how to handle it for the most part. When a patient presents with a low potassium level on lab work, we give supplemental potassium and check another lab to ensure that the potassium had been replenished to an adequate level within normal limits. With regard to pain, there really is no objective way to check the presence or severity of a patient's pain. We, as physicians, must rely on a subjective description of the pain in order to evaluate it. As a medical student, I would ask patients to rank their pain level from 0-10 with 0 being the absence of pain and 10 being the most excruciating pain ever felt and they would commonly answer 12 or 13, occasionally 20 or, as has happened once, 103! Now, having been in their shoes, I think I understand why patients do this. Physicians tend to not pay close attention to the answer. If a patient says 3-4, it is assumed the patient has no pain at all. If they answer 8-10, the physician assumes that we should give them pain meds until the level comes down to an acceptable level, that is 5-6. But what if the pain truly is unbearable, what does a patient say? 10 obviously won't get the attention needed, so 13 is tried instead in hopes that someone will notice and do something, anything, to help. I was of the opinion that no matter how much pain I personally experienced, it could always be worse, so I routinely answered 7 for what I qualified as "straight pain."

Without the opioids, my body would refuse to breathe. The simple action of taking more than shallow breaths triggered such severe pain from my ribs and back that my body turned down the very core instinct of life that is breathing. I called it breath-taking pain because quite literally, it was.

I realized that my body had become physiologically dependent on opioids when I had to take 15mg of oxycodone every 3 hours to prevent profuse sweating and discomfort in my back. Not knowing any better, I had, in the first few months following my hospital discharge, continued certain medications including baclofen that was supposed to control my involuntary leg spasms, oxybutynin supposed to control urinary bladder spasms and incontinence, and opioid therapies supposed to control my pain. I wasn't sure the baclofen and oxybutynin worked at all, and it became clear to me that the opioids' only benefit was in curbing withdrawal effects. In September 2006, I decided that I would wean myself off opioids entirely. In a matter of days, I cut down the dose of the oxycodone from 15mg orally every three hours, to 10mg, then down to 5mg, and then stopped. This was a very aggressive taper which is perhaps not the way most physicians would suggest a taper be carried out, but it worked for me. My pain level increased for a couple of days and I sweated heavily as part of the physiological withdrawal, but by the end of the week, I was off opioids completely and have never again taken another opioid pill. Around the same time, I realized that if I stayed in bed on a Sunday morning, I experienced more pain than on the days when I got up early and got moving. The supine position in bed exacerbated not only the pain in my right shoulder where I had impingement syndrome, but also in my back. It became evident that exercise and movement were the best medicine against pain and I started working out daily with a paramount functional trainer machine, which was located in the gym of my apartment building, to optimize the function in my arms and significantly reduce my pain level. Over time, I was able to rehabilitate my right shoulder and recover a high level of physical fitness.

Daily Struggles

Living alone meant that I had to be able to care for myself and perform my own grocery shopping. Fortunately, Smith's Marketplace, a large grocery store carrying everything one might ever need, was located only a couple of city blocks away from my apartment, across the busy 4th South street which, in addition to three car lanes on each side, had rails for the tram in the center. Traversing the rails was exquisitely tricky as I had to pop a wheelie and lift the front casters, the small front wheels of a wheelchair, to prevent them from dropping into the rails' gaps, four consecutive times. The timing of the wheelies had to be just right as I moved swiftly through the multiple lanes and over the tracks during the short countdown between green lights. Once, a well-meaning woman tried to help by pushing me across 4th South, and by doing so, interfered with my regular pace and timing for the wheelies resulting in the planting of the casters into the Tram's rails. Of course, once the casters were locked in the rails, the momentum of the continued push against the back rest caused the chair to tip forward effectively dumping me on the tracks in front of the Tram. The kind woman couldn't have been more embarrassed. A driver got out of his car to help her carry me back into the wheelchair. Propelling a wheelchair by pushing on the rear wheels causes the front casters to offload from the floor allowing me to go, albeit, not without effort, over grass, dirt or packed sand. Alternatively, having someone push me from the back increases the load onto the casters causing them to dig into the ground creating a fulcrum and, as exemplified in the episode with the tram rails, continuing to push simply tilts the chair forward and dumps me out.

I often explain to people that while their offer to help is always appreciated, I am so accustomed to certain aspects of my life in a wheelchair that unfortunately, their good intentions to assist can in fact hinder an otherwise smooth and well-rehearsed process which can ultimately be detrimental. The best example of this is perhaps getting the wheelchair in the car. People always want to help, standing over the chair, trying to move it this way or that way and trying to remove wheels when they don't know how, and essentially, they are just getting in the way. I basically have learned to explain, as politely as I can, after thanking them for their kindness and good intentions, that the best way they could help me is by taking a step back and letting me carry out the process of getting the chair in the car unassisted in a methodical and efficient manner.

Every once in a while, the interactions I have with people, while not meant to be humorous at the time, can turn out to be quite funny in retrospect if you are equipped with a good sense of humor and don't take people's comments too seriously. On one occasion, while grabbing some milk at the grocery store, I was approached by a woman who said: "Seeing people like you in wheelchairs makes me mad!" I slowly looked over to her, unsure of what to make of what she had just said. While I was deliberating about whether or not to answer, she added: "My neighbor's nephew has the same thing you have, but he worked very hard in rehab and now, he can walk again, so I know that the only reason you are in this chair is because you are lazy!" I marveled at her ability to construct such an illogical sentence, felt bad for her, smiled, and went back to my grocery shopping without saying anything back because I felt too lazy to answer.

A Family Visit

My aunt and uncle Veronique and Patrick went on a cruise in Alaska in June 2006, and before returning to France, had arranged to fly to Salt Lake City to visit me for a couple of days. It was very nice to see them and I was touched that they would make the detour to see me. While I had initially told my mom not to come visit me in the first few months after my accident as I did not want her to see me struggle, by August 2006, I felt as though I had a good grip on life and my mom could schedule a visit. She and my brother David came for a week at the end of October. I remember driving to the airport to pick them up and felt so proud that I had been able to regain my independence. We drove to Bryce Canyon, one of my all-time favorite places in the world, then down to Saint George and eventually worked our way to Las Vegas. I had booked a room at the Bellagio and was very happy to be able to take my mom there for a short vacation. While it was the last week in October, the weather was gorgeous and I remember eating an idyllic lunch by the pool. As a souvenir, I bought my mom the full tourist panoply which included Bellagio sweat pants and a Bellagio t-shirt. Our room at the Bellagio was the very first fully handicap accessible room I had seen outside of a healthcare facility. It was not only luxurious in the proper sense of the term, it was also beautifully thought-out for someone in a wheelchair. We "walked" up and down the strip. Overall, while the vacation only lasted a week, we had a lovely time together. We drove back to Salt Lake and right upon arriving, I had my first flat tire on the wheelchair. A flat tire on a wheelchair is equivalent to a broken ankle in someone who can walk. It stops you in your tracks instantly. Fortunately, I had a set of spare wheels at home. Had the flat happened on the Vegas strip, I would have been in a heap of trouble and I thanked my lucky star that it only happened upon our return home. I made a point to always remind my friends and patients in the wheelchair community to be prepared with a spare wheel that could be switched as needed in the event of a flat. There are other downsides of inflated tires. Wheelchair brakes work by applying pressure to the outside of the tire and this requires tires to be fully pumped. The constant, progressive, albeit minor deflation of the tires which is a normal occurrence, renders brakes less effective as the tire pressure drops and the overall diameter of the wheel decreases ever so slightly. One always needs to remember to pump up the tires which isn't easy to do when sitting in the wheelchair. Consequently, after a while, I learned about foam tires which are maintenance-free and cannot get flat and I have been using them ever since.

I was very pleased to have had the opportunity to show my mom what my daily routine was like and show her that I could get by on my own so that she wouldn't have to worry needlessly about me. Clearly, I had suffered a bump in the road, but it was water under the bridge and while difficult, the road ahead would not be impossible.

Susan Sample, the Professor leading the poetry group I had been a part of right upon my hospital discharge was also the Editor of the University of Utah Health Sciences Report. She proposed that a piece be written about me in the report, which would also provide an opportunity for some of the poetry I had written to be published. A photo shoot was scheduled with Sean Graff while my brother and mother were in town and we ended up with beautiful family pictures taken in Liberty Park in Salt Lake City.

The first day of snow in the fall of 2006 happened the night before David and my mom went home. While snow used to bring a smile to my face, this time, it brought tears to my eyes. David, my mother, my neighbor and friend Monica Rojas and I were eating dinner at Su Casa, the Mexican restaurant neighboring our apartment building, and while looking at the snow gently floating through the air, I wondered how I would carry on, propelling my wheelchair in the snowy streets by myself. New challenges would come up, one at a time and would need to be handled. As Dr. Elizabeth Allen had taught me during my hospitalization, there was no need to worry about tomorrow and the best way to tackle those challenges was to do it, one at a time, as they presented themselves. Certainly, I expected that situations would arise in the upcoming months and years that would not be easy, but the resiliency that had served me well in other aspects of my life would surely get me through most anything.

CHAPTER 18

INTERNAL MEDICINE INTERNSHIP

I officially graduated from medical school in December 2006 instead of June 2006, having been delayed by my accident and subsequent hospitalization. In order to provide me with the health insurance I desperately needed within the first year of my paralysis, Dr. Caroline Milne, Program Director of the Internal Medicine Internship and Residency Training Program arranged for me to start my post-doctoral training in February 2007 instead of the customary July 1st starting date. I was very grateful to be the recipient of such a generous accommodation even though I still occasionally joke that while the intern year is the hardest, most demanding year of medical training, mine lasted 18 months instead of 12 and I completed it after having recently been paralyzed. Here is what I mean by demanding: We would work 80hrs a week and when on call, we would show up at 6am one day and go home at 1pm the next day. Since, the rules have drastically changed and a night call rotation has been added so that nobody has to work such long shifts which could be unfavorable to the optimal delivery of patient care.

While I rotated between LDS hospital, the University of Utah Hospital and the George E. Wahlen VA Medical Center in Salt Lake City, most of my rotations were at the VA, where I had been given my own room and attached bathroom on one side of the internal medicine unit so that I could rest and shower when on call. The "year" went by very fast. I had become accustomed to my new physical limitations, worked very long hours, visited the gym daily, and overall, while I did encounter significant difficulties, I did not have much time to feel sorry for myself. Also, very early on, I had met a patient who had lost the use of his arms and, at a time when I was personally mourning the loss of my legs, that patient said to me: "You look very fit, I wish I had your arms." Right there and then I pondered: Who am I to feel sorry for myself when others have less than I have and can be envious of me? My whole life I had wished I had been a little bit taller or better looking, and after my accident I wished that I had been paralyzed lower in the thoracic spine so that I could still have the use of my abs. I think it is human nature to always want a little more, but I learned that the key to happiness is not found looking for things we do not have or things we cannot change. Happiness, instead, is found in the contentment with, and the gratefulness for, the things that we do have. I had lost the use of my legs, but I still had my brain, my arms, and with a positive attitude, I could continue to strive.

RETURN TO SKIING

After the one-year anniversary of my accident, Dr. Schmidt cleared me to resume intense athletic activity. Essentially, I was cleared to return to skiing if I so wished.

Prior to this I had flown to Reno to spend some time with my friend Holly McGowan in Truckee, who introduced me to adapted cross country skiing and took me to meet the man who had custom-built her cross-country sleigh. He took my measurements and built me a cross country sleigh with custom-fit bucket seat. I purchased Atomic cross-country skis, and poles had to be chopped down to be adapted to use from a seated position. Cross-country skiing seemed less dangerous than downhill skiing and I had felt safe enough to start within the first year of my accident. My friend, professional mountain bike downhill racer Chris Van Dine took me to Millcreek Canyon for the inauguration of this new exciting piece of equipment. It took me an hour to cover one mile, uphill. I had never breathed so heavily in my life. It was the most physically demanding activity I had ever done. Just imagine a sleigh without breaks, aimed uphill, where the sole source of power to propel forward is one's arms. If I took a break, I still somehow had to hold the sleigh in place by maintaining the poles firmly stuck into the snow to prevent the rig from sliding backwards down the hill. I enjoyed being outdoors and was very happy to reconnect with the mountains, but clearly, this activity was not a walk in the park and would be better fitted to flat lands. Even the way down was a bit treacherous as I really had no way to steer or brake and nearly ended up in the creek below.

Having been cleared to participate in more intense activities like downhill skiing, I couldn't wait to get started, since after all, nothing could be more intense than my climb up Millcreek canyon.

That's when I got a call from Peter Mandler, the founder of Wasatch Adaptive Sports at Snowbird. He graciously invited me to come up so that he and his group of specialized instructors could teach me how to sit-ski. Peter is a very altruistic man, one of those people who dedicate their lives to helping others. He is the Mother Theresa of adaptive sports and spearheaded the adaptive program at Snowbird resort since 1977.

My feelings were mixed during my first day back on the slopes of Snowbird. I got teary eyed thinking about the giant step back my accident forced me to take, but at the same time, the overwhelming kindness of the people who assisted me throughout the day warmed up my heart. I started on a dual ski in the "bowl." The bowl is an area for little kids to play on, and there is a "magic carpet" that brings one up the slope. Interestingly enough, the bowl was so flat that I wasn't sure which way was down and which way was up. I stayed there for about 30 minutes. I think it is much easier to stay balanced with some incline and some speed rather than on a flat surface, but we needed to start somewhere, so there I was on the easy version of the bunny hill. Soon, I was upgraded to the "real" bunny hill. The equipment unfortunately was not adequate, and my upper body was not well supported. My entire weight was resting on my half-bent arms and I experienced deadly cramps while at the same time trying to focus on maintaining my balance and initiating turns. After a couple of hours, I switched to using another sit ski called the "Yeti racer." This one turned out to be much better. My positioning was improved and overall, it afforded me a more comfortable ride and I could focus on my technique. I rode this Yeti racer for another hour and progressed quite a bit in only a few runs.

I used to leap over boulders, but that day, I was taking precarious and insecure baby steps on the bunny hill. What a change!

There was something beautiful about this whole experience. Usually, I would go ride on my own and spend the whole day riding by myself. Few of my friends in medical school shared my passion for snowboarding and I would frequently go ride alone. That first day on a sit-ski however, marked a new day. It was different. One skier was holding a tether line behind me, one skier was on my side, another one was skiing backwards in front of me to guide me and counsel me on proper technique, and another person was there to record the experience on camera. Two of my friends were there also with video and still cameras. I was surrounded by people who cared about me, people whose sole purpose that day was to help me, people, some of whom I had never met before but who, on this day, were dedicated to making sure I had a wonderful experience. These are special people with a huge heart. Peter Mandler, Brian Jupina, David Watson, David Schoeneck, Laura Cantin, Chris Van Dine, Emily Hagn all make the world a better place. So many people cared, I was truly overwhelmed with emotions and no matter how much I struggled, nothing could have erased the grin on my face. I know I looked awkward on that bunny slope, yet they cheered me on as if I was charging for a gold medal in the Winter Olympic Games.

Even though I felt like crying while thinking about how much I used to carve the hill on a snowboard, my heart rejoiced knowing that I had made so many new friends. Circumstances had changed. I was no longer riding like I used to, but at least I wasn't alone. I spent the day surrounded by genuinely awesome people, and who knew, maybe someday I would skillfully carve the hill again, in a sit ski.

I was always happy to lend a hand to any and all fundraising activities organized by Wasatch Adaptive Sports. On April 17th, 2007, Peter Mandler asked me if I could be at Snowbird by 5am to, along with other sit-skiers, demo this adapted sport for Al Roker of the Today Show. We had to be on the snow early to accommodate the broadcasting of the show at 7am Eastern Standard Time. After the demo, I joined Peter Mandler and Al Roker on the Snowbird Plaza for a quick interview. Al Roker had brought the show's "Lend a Hand" tour to Utah to make very generous donations to Wasatch Adaptive Sports. Among the donations that had been made possible through The Today Show and its charitable sponsors, were all sorts of skiing equipment for children, snow pants, jackets, helmets, goggles, as well as office supplies and even a sport utility vehicle to transport the equipment wherever needed for lessons. The amount of donations bestowed upon the program and the kindness it reflected were nothing short of overwhelming. Soon after, while rotating through the neurology clinic, I met a young boy with Duchenne Muscular Dystrophy, a disease that causes progressive muscle weakening and almost invariably leads to the person's premature death in the late 20s in the majority of cases. The cost of his medical care had been such that it did not leave his family with a lot of means for recreational activities. I inquired if he had ever tried skiing. He answered that other kids at school sometimes went skiing on the week-end but that he himself, while he would have loved to try, had never had the chance. Thanks to Wasatch Adaptive Sports, Snowbird resort and The Today Show, we were able to change that. I referred him and his mom to go see Peter at Snowbird, to be fully outfitted with ski clothes and partake in skiing lessons, absolutely free of charge. It was a beautiful and joyful moment for me to be able to refer this boy to an activity I knew he would tremendously enjoy and I remembered the words spoken years earlier by Richard D. King, who said that the person who benefits the most from serving others is the person providing the help. Clearly, as in this case, the satisfaction that comes from giving, can be equal to, if not be greater than, the satisfaction that comes from receiving.

CHAPTER 19

THE WHEELCHAIR WORKOUT AND THE YOUTUBE CHANNEL

Ever since my time at BYU, I had made it a priority to work out at least an hour a day, and often more, in addition to participating in sports such as racquetball, swimming, diving or snowboarding. After being paralyzed, it was undeniable that some adaptations needed to take place in order for me to remain active. Fortunately, the apartment building I lived in had a brand-new gym with a Paramount Functional Trainer with articulated arms which, with a little bit of creativity, allowed me to design an exercise program fitted to my particular needs. By moving the articulated arms in specific positions, I was able to strengthen my arms, my shoulders, my pecs and my upper back. While in my intern year, despite a busy work schedule, I tried to work out most days of the week. My friends at the time mentioned that it would be great if somehow I could find a way to show other patients with paraplegia how I worked out.

YouTube was in its early stages, and, as I struggled to find information relevant to life as a person with paraplegia, and wanted to find a way to carry my own message to the world, on February 14th, 2007, I created my own YouTube channel: "A paraplegic's life." It wasn't going to be a popular or particularly entertaining channel, but if through it, I could reach a single person in need of information, inspiration or motivation, it would be a success in my eyes.

The first two videos I uploaded onto the channel were of my fourth lesson of sit skiing at Snowbird with Wasatch Adaptive Sport. My friend Emily Hagn had done the filming. Watching those videos now, I can't help but be impressed by how comfortable I looked after only a handful of hours of practice. I thought it would be fun for people to see that I had made it back to Snowbird only a year after having sustained a life altering accident. I didn't want my last memory at a ski resort to be anxiety provoking and it was important for me to conquer my fears and return to Snowbird to create new memories, happy memories, to show that life does go on. On the second-year anniversary of my accident, I went sit skiing and made a video titled: "Gael's 2-year Anniversary" filmed by Peter Mandler, and soon after, on a beautiful April afternoon, in a video called: "Just another afternoon on the hill…" I returned precisely to the run where my accident had taken place, to, as my friend Dave Schoeneck put it at the end of the video, "conquer my nemesis."

Since my workout had triggered the desire and initiative to share my ideas and methods with others, I endeavored to put together a short video titled: "Paraplegic workout routine." My friend and fellow wheelchair user, Stan Clawson a talented videographer, helped with the filming and I edited the video on my own, learning how to do it on the fly. To date, my paraplegic workout routine is the most viewed video on the topic on YouTube.

Over the ensuing two years, I posted a video explaining how I had gotten paralyzed and other videos showing me involved in various activities such as bowling, handcycling uphill at Snowbird, snowmobiling, sand yachting in France, getting in and out of a pool, kayaking in a pool, getting dressed, transferring to the floor from a wheelchair and back up, transferring in and out of a car, transferring to a shower bench, getting dressed and performing house chores. Essentially, I put up videos of whatever I thought people would benefit from watching. Often, I filmed the videos myself with a camcorder and a tripod, but occasionally, friends, like previously mentioned Stan Clawson or Dr. Lee Kneer helped with the filming. After only 26 videos in total, I ran out of ideas of interesting things to show and stopped making videos, but the videos I had made during those two years continue to be watched daily throughout the world.

After over ten years, I am astounded by the reach of those informal, modest videos on the topic of living with paraplegia. The YouTube analytics demonstrated that over one million people across the world have watched my few short videos, in excess of 360,000 minutes in total as of December 2018. That is as if a single person had watched my videos, back to back for 40 hours per week for about 3 years.

The majority of my viewers originate from the United States, are between 25 and 34 years of age, are men, and access my videos from a mobile phone. While this information is interesting, the most exciting part, in my opinion, is that the rest of the data provided by the YouTube Analytics shows that people of all genders throughout the entire age spectrum have watched my videos from over 50 countries and territories including Germany, United Kingdom, France, Canada, Taiwan, Brazil, Spain, Japan, Mexico, Australia, Italy, Indonesia, New Zealand, South Korea, India, Czechia, Vietnam, Norway, Netherlands, Thailand, Russia, Sweden, Croatia, Switzerland, Philippines, Austria, Belgium, Singapore, Poland, Greece, Colombia, Argentina, Turkey, Denmark, Hong Kong, Dominican Republic, Egypt, South Africa, Hungary, Malaysia, Portugal, Finland, Morocco, Romania, Serbia, Jordan, Nigeria, Brunei and Slovakia. Reading that list never ceases to amaze me and I am humbled to think that thanks to YouTube I have been able to reach people from all over the world. Early on, I received a very kind email from a woman in India, thanking me for putting up those videos as they helped her brother deal with a new paralysis. As I mentioned earlier, if I could help but one person, it would make my modest presence on YouTube worthwhile, so I was humbled and happy to have been of some help.

A couple of years later I received another email, from Germany, asking me for permission to use my videos for a psychology class at the University from a lovely young woman who would later become my wife.

CHAPTER 20

PHYSICAL MEDICINE AND REHABILITATION RESIDENCY PART 1

At the term of my intern year, after passing yet another grueling medical licensing examination (USMLE Step 3), I transitioned into a residency program in Physical Medicine and Rehabilitation (PM&R) at the University of Utah. PM&R is the branch of medicine that endeavors to optimize functional ability and quality of life for those, such as myself, with physical impairments or disabilities.

I rotated between the University of Utah hospital, the VA hospital, Salt Lake Regional Medical Center and Primary Children's Hospital. Each month would focus on a different area of care such as stroke, traumatic brain injury, spinal cord injury, cerebral palsy etc... I felt as though my personal experience with the field of PM&R, as a patient, only two years prior, gave me a peculiar understanding of the emotional aspect of encountering a disability for the first time, and this, I believe, facilitated building a rapport with patients whose care had been entrusted to me. During that time, patients, specifically those with spinal cord injuries, were not simply patients and a lot became friends because we had something undeniable in common.

In France and other European countries, motorcyclists have a "code of conduct" to identify themselves as part of a tight community. Every time motorcyclists cross paths, they lift their left hand from the handlebars to say hello. Also, if a motorcyclist is stranded on the side of the road, inevitably, the next motorcyclist driving by will stop to lend a hand. I find the wheelchair community to be remarkably similar. When cruising anywhere, whether it be in Europe or in America, it seems that whenever I encounter another person in a wheelchair, I wave, nod and smile as a sign of acknowledgement and they do the same to me. Also, frequently, if the circumstances are conducive to it, we engage in conversation with one another. I find that I have met a lot of wheelchair users because of this habit. One of those people is Randy Curry, a man I randomly met in the parking lot of the hospital. We started talking about cars and exchanged methods on how to load and unload chairs. On the spot, he invited me to dinner to meet his wife Stacey. Both were dedicated tennis players and played several days a week. In fact, Stacey, a realtor, found time to play almost daily. They introduced me to wheelchair tennis and the concept of "Up and Down" which is when one person standing, teams up with one wheelchair user on each side of the court. I was able to borrow a tennis chair and played about 4 hours a week and really enjoyed it. Randy was an elite tennis player who had been involved in the sport for a long time, knew a lot of people and introduced me to even more wheelchair tennis players, further widening my circle of friends in the wheelchair community in which I had been adopted. While Randy and I played tennis in the spring, summer and fall, I introduced him to skiing in the winter, which activity he picked up with a lot of enthusiasm.

Through my athletic activities and involvement with specialized groups such as Snowbird's based Wasatch Adaptive Sports, I came across a lot of Paralympians, Olympians, and other athletes. Eventually, I was invited to join the Board of Directors of Wasatch Adaptive Sports alongside, among others, Steve Young, Chad Lewis, Bob Bonar, Peter Mandler and Stefani Kimche, and continued to share my positive experience with this organization whenever the need arose.

The owner of Snowbird resort was a man named Dick Bass, who was the first man to climb the "Seven Summits," that is, the highest mountains on each continent. Him and I shared a birthday date of December 21st. Each year, I was invited to speak a few words on behalf of Wasatch Adaptive Sports during the celebration of his birthday at Snowbird during an event called "The Summit Gala" which doubled as a fundraiser for Snowbird and its benevolent activities. It was one of the two main events during which money was raised to support charitable programs such as Wasatch Adaptive Sports. During one of the birthday parties, a video was displayed where Dick's friends, one after another, read a line from the poem "If" by Rudyard Kipling. This brought to my attention the fact that he was a poetry lover and I learned that he had a lot of poems memorized, which he used to recite to himself while climbing. Consequently, the next year, with that in mind, after taking the stage in front of over three hundred guests as a spokesperson for Wasatch Adaptive Sports, I recited to him "Invictus" by William Ernest Henley. As I recited the poem, I watched him mouth every word from memory. He was an extraordinary man who died in 2015 at the age of 85.

In addition to "The Summit Gala," the main fundraiser in support of Wasatch Adaptive Sports was, and still is, "The Steve Young Ski Classic" named after Steve Young, the legendary Hall of Fame NFL quarterback. The first edition of the fundraiser took place in 1986 and has been going strong ever since. The Steve Young Ski Classic was routinely attended by many celebrities in the sports arena, including NFL players, NBA players, football coaches from BYU and the University of Utah, Paralympians and Olympians.

One year, Chris Langeland told me that, as he was watching the news without paying close attention to the television, he heard my distinctive laugh, looked up and saw Steve Young and I being interviewed. The following year, I invited Chris to the fundraiser so that he could meet Steve Young. Chris was awestruck and very happy to have the opportunity to chat with Steve, with whom he took a selfie and had the picture as a background on his computer for many years. I love how famous athletes and celebrities in general for that matter have the ability to make people feel special and happy just by being around them.

Through "The Steve Young Ski Classic" I had the wonderful opportunity to meet Paralympic athletes and role models Chris Waddell, Muffy Davis and Tanja Kari. Chris Waddell is a wheelchair racer and skier, five-time Paralympian and Paralympic Gold medalist who has won medals in both the summer and winter Paralympic Games. Muffy Davis is a skier and handcyclist, three-time Paralympian and Paralympic Gold medalist who has also won medals in both the summer and winter Paralympic Games. Tanya Kari is a cross-country skier, four-time Paralympian and Gold Medalist in the winter Paralympic games. The number of Paralympic medals these three phenomenal athletes have amassed throughout their careers is simply mind boggling. I strongly encourage you to look them up on Wikipedia for details. I also met Bill Demong, Nordic combined skier, five-time Olympian and Olympic Gold medalist. Finally, last but not least, I met extreme skier, climber and high endurance athlete John Collinson who was the youngest person to summit the seven summits.

Meeting and mingling with all these amazing athletes motivated and inspired me to continue my own modest athletic endeavors as a weekend warrior through skiing, tennis and handcycling.

Dr. Zach Beresford was a resident in the year ahead of me in residency. Hailing from Minnesota, he was a wonderful cross-country skier and a very kind human being. After learning of my experience with adapted cross-country skiing and the significant difficulties the uphill portions presented, he and his father thought of attaching a bungee cord between Zack and me so that he could pull me up and facilitate the ascents when needed. His father sent him the cord and we went to try it out at Soldier Hollow, the cross-country venue for the Salt Lake Olympic Games. It worked beautifully! While individually, I would have been able to push myself through a portion of the course, having Zack by my side, pulling me through the challenging portions, amplified the distance traveled, and thanks to his support, I was able to go places I wouldn't have been able to reach on my own. The same is true in life. We can always reach certain goals independently, but it is only through the help of others during challenging times that we can achieve goals that would have otherwise been unreachable.

Toward the end of my first year of PM&R residency I decided to contact Dr. William Close to take him up on his invitation to visit him, his wife Bettine and their many dogs in Big Piney, Wyoming. Unfortunately, my call came too late as he had passed away only two weeks prior. I was very sad. I had allowed a busy schedule to get in the way of visiting a one of a kind physician whose life I was very familiar with, having read all of the books he had written and whom I had grown to admire since I had met him at the beginning of medical school. I had missed an opportunity to get to know him better on a personal level. Sometimes we get so caught up in our day to day life that we miss out on once in a lifetime opportunities.

One morning, as I was about to go to work at Primary's Children Hospital, I found Calypso, my youngest baby rabbit curled on the floor hidden in my closet. This was an unusual place for her as she usually slept nestled against Edonis. I carefully picked her up and found her to be limp and weak. I rested her on my lap as I petted her and wrapped her in a soft wool sweater. I grabbed my stethoscope to listen to her while she was cuddled against me and literally, as I was listening to her heart beat, it stopped. This was a terrifyingly heartbreaking experience. I was so overwhelmed by sadness that I couldn't speak. I couldn't call the chief resident to explain that I wouldn't be coming in to work so I just texted to explain what had occurred. Later that day, my friend Dr. Lee Kneer and his wife Cara, drove Calypso and me to Silver Lake by Brighton resort so we could find her a beautiful resting place.

CHAPTER 21

PHYSICAL MEDICINE AND REHABILITATION RESIDENCY PART 2

In the summer, I used an adaptive bike called the One-Off to climb mountain trails around Snowbird. After building up my endurance with highly demanding physical expenditure at altitude, on October 1st, 2009, I was the first person to climb to the summit of Hidden Peak at 11,000 feet starting from Snowbird's base, representing some 3,000 feet of vertical climb, in 6 hours and 45 minutes using solely my arms' strength. I use this climb frequently in motivational speeches as it is the perfect example of a seemingly impossible task at first, that gets accomplished, little by little, through hard work and perseverance. Standing on the Snowbird plaza, by the base of the tram, one cannot even see the Hidden Peak tram terminal. It is only after a few hours of relentless uphill pedaling that one gets a glimpse of the target. I find that looking at goals too far ahead, while essential for long term planning, can also be discouraging if not linked with the reward of reaching smaller steps and celebrating small victories along the way. While my goal was unequivocally to reach 11,000 feet, I divided this ultimate goal into smaller, less intimidating ones, to initially reach the first turn in the trail, then the second and the third and so forth. Little by little, I worked my way up the hill, stopping every once in a while, for a few seconds, to look back and gain appreciation for the distance already covered. The last 2 hours of the climb were the most physically demanding. By then, my neck, my chest and my arms were hurting significantly from the constant effort and the positioning on the bike. My right forearm was especially painful, so much so in fact that I thought I might have suffered a stress fracture in my radius or my ulna. I could have quit at any time and rolled down the hill, but I was determined to reach my goal, no matter the cost. I persevered in spite of the mounting pain, kept my head down and enjoyed the small victories, one yard at a time. I kept pushing forward. As I came around the last turn in the trail, I was exhausted but finally had the tram terminal in direct sight, just one hundred yards away. On the terminal platform, three Alpenhorn players acted as the welcoming committee. Adults and children gathered around me to provide encouragement for the final uphill battle. I was beat and felt like catching my breath and resting my aching upper body after each pedal rotation, but given the circumstances, the fact that people were videotaping me and were cheering me on over the final stretch, I couldn't possibly rest, so I pushed on, unremittingly. Finally, I reached 11,000 ft. I was elated, and looking out to the valley below, I savored the sense of accomplishment that comes from reaching a worthy goal through sustained hard work.

The pain in my right forearm was severe and was exacerbated by any movement of the wrist. It was diagnosed as Intersection Syndrome from overactivity and

I had to wear a soft immobilizing wrist splint for the following two weeks which, surprisingly, did not significantly damper my ability to propel my wheelchair. Since every cloud has a silver lining and I believe in making the best of a situation, I used the opportunity to learn all there was to know about this condition and wrote an article titled: "Intersection Syndrome in a Handcyclist: A Case Report and Literature Review" which was published in the medical journal Topics in Spinal Cord Injury Rehabilitation.

It was around the middle of my residency that I was given a special and unusual gift: Elon, my first service dog. I had traveled to San Diego to be introduced to Elon and be taught how to properly care for him. At the term of the two weeks of on-site training, Brooks Rohlen flew in to attend the graduation ceremony, during which I gave a speech, having been made the spokesperson for the group of graduating students. It was overall a wonderful and happy day.

Soon after, Elon and I visited Brooks at his condo in Squaw Valley in California and Brooks' dog Primo taught Elon what he hadn't learned in the service dog curriculum, that is, how to jump paws first into a mountain pond!

Elon was a beautiful lab retriever mix who had a truly positive energy about him and stole my heart at first sight. He was adventurous, always eager to go places and I thought he blended perfectly with my active lifestyle in the hospital and in the mountains. He rounded daily by my side in the Neurology and Rehabilitation units of the University of Utah during the week and eagerly hiked trails at Snowbird on the week-end. He had his own Snowbird picture identification and was in dog heaven, running the alpine trails while faking to chase chipmunks and marmots. Because having Elon on a leash at all times while performing my duties as a physician in the hospital or while handcycling at Snowbird was simply not feasible, and because he never left my side anyway, I got in the habit of letting him be free in those two environments which, combined, represented the vast majority of the places we visited. Elon was essentially only leashed while walking to the grocery store because we had to cross a busy street, and because of this, I only kept his leash at home. One night, when arriving at a fund raiser for the National Ability Center in Park City, I realized that I had forgotten to bring Elon's leash and decided to join the event anyway, trusting that Elon would stay by my side, which he did for the most part, only occasionally getting distracted by mouth-watering smells from appetizers served to guests prior to dinner. He was overall very well behaved and I was proud of him.

As it turned out, one of the guests at the event contacted the company that had trained Elon to notify them that they had seen him off-leash. They might have also seen Elon get a morsel of steak from the dinner, both of which, while they didn't seem like outrageous offenses to me at the time, were clearly against the rules as outlined by the company. Consequently, an investigation was launched, and through a quick review of social media accounts, it was revealed that Elon was in fact mostly off-leash in the hospital and in the mountains. Certainly, I was at fault in all of this as I should have followed the clearly defined rules to a T but I didn't. Following the heavy set of rules, to me, meant that I needed to act as a drill sergeant with an iron fist, and instead, my personal inclination was to be a loving companion with a petting hand. After 18 months of us being inseparable, I came to understand that the rules had not been meant to be subject to my interpretation when Elon was abruptly taken from me because of my inability to follow them. The heavily mediatized ordeal that ensued was one of the most stressful and heartbreaking part of my life. The story took a life of its own on social media with thousands of people getting involved. Eventually, the company, having deemed my lifestyle to be endangering Elon's well-being, stood by their decision not to return him to me. While this reasoning didn't make sense to me as I had always thought my lifestyle to be perfect for a young active dog, what did make sense is that I had not followed rules and a price had to be paid. While I obviously wished the outcome had been different, I wholly understand my responsibility in how the events unfolded and my failure to comply with rules did indeed lead me to pay a most hefty price.

In the latter portion of my residency, as I was removing my undershirt while seated in my wheelchair, I momentarily became simultaneously blinded and entangled with the shirt over my head, lost my balance and toppled over the side of the chair, unable to catch myself, landing square on the crown of my head. I felt an immediate crack from the traumatic impact with the hard floor. I lay immobile for a few minutes, with tingling sensations in my hands, stunned and worried that I might have caused further neurological damage to my spinal cord. I knew the impact was likely to have caused a disc bulge in my cervical spine that would compress the nerve roots of the nerves traveling to my hands, but I was hoping the crack I had heard didn't mean I would need to return under the knife. I slowly and methodically completed a cursory neurological self-examination to find out that, aside from the tingling sensation, I seemed to have no other neurological deficits. I drove myself to the University of Utah where I underwent a CT scan of the neck where I was confident the damage had occurred. To my surprise and relief, there was no fracture noted in my cervical spine. The source of the cracking sound would be revealed 5 months later as an incidental finding during routine post-surgical follow-up imaging.

CHAPTER 22

PHYSICAL MEDICINE AND REHABILITATION RESIDENCY PART 3

After losing my dog Elon, I went through a period of severe depression and distracted myself from the emotional pain by increasing my participation in sports.

With the support of Wasatch Adaptive Sports, I was able to participate in the Park City portion of the Larry H. Miller Tour of Utah. Will Lachenauer from Reno, Nevada also made his debut in handcycling during the Tour of Utah, and he obliterated the field and lapped me a couple of times while going uphill on Main Street in Park City. His speed was far superior than anybody else's that day. While I kept my day job, Will went on to become a World Champion handcyclist and a Paralympic athlete competing in the Summer Paralympic Games in Rio de Janeiro. I cannot stress enough what serious athletes Paralympians are, as they truly are an elite group. Not infrequently, when people learn that I casually participate in sports, they ask me if I have participated in the Paralympic games. I have been asked this question so often that I believe there is a widespread misconception that anybody in a wheelchair could just show up to the Paralympic games and be handed a medal for participation, when in fact, this couldn't be further from the truth. Every time I get asked the question of whether my casual participation in sports had landed me a spot in the Paralympic games, I use the opportunity to explain that the selection process and dedication required to become a Paralympian for a disabled athlete, is as difficult and grueling as the selection process and dedication required to become an Olympian for a non-disabled athlete. Essentially, it would be equivalent to me asking someone who likes to play basketball on the weekend if he or she had ever competed in the Olympic games. I have heard the wonderful comedian and my fellow BYU graduate Ryan Hamilton, in his stand-up special Happy Face, say that we should always put a regular guy in the pool next to Michael Phelps so that viewers could fully appreciate how much better an elite Olympic athlete is, compared to average Joe. Similarly, they should put me in the handcycling races in the Paralympic games so people could truly appreciate what tremendous athletes Paralympians are in comparison. While we are on the topic, allow me to illustrate with an example. A lot of my friends in Salt Lake City are cycling enthusiasts. On Saturdays, a few of them ride up Emigration Canyon and the more valiant in the group would push all the way to Big Mountain Pass, up UT-65 way above Little Dell Reservoir, which I have occasionally done with them in a handcycle. My able-bodied friends and I feel good about our level of fitness for being able to accomplish this feat. I have met Derek Para, Olympic Gold Medalist in speed skating through Josh Romney and learned that for exercise, Derek would cycle down from Park City to the Salt Lake valley, then up Little Cottonwood Canyon, then up Big

Cottonwood Canyon and back up Parley's Canyon to Park City. So, effectively, you can see that there is "average Joe fitness" and there is "Olympic fitness" and they are completely different from one another. In conclusion, the difference in fitness between Will Lachenauer, Muffy Davis, Chris Waddell, Tanya Kari, as a group, and myself, is the same as the difference in fitness between any average week-end cyclist and the likes of Michael Phelps and Derek Para.

While I had never thought of running a marathon before getting paralyzed, I thought that entering one on a handcycle might be fun. Like regular bicycles, the type of handcycles used to climb a mountain is drastically different from the type used in road racing or marathons. The handcycle used to climb hills has two wheels in the front and one wheel in the back. Turning the front wheels is achieved via the pivoting of a chest plate on which a kneeling person rests their sternum while pedaling. When not pedaling, the front wheels can be turned via the use of a handlebar. The pedals are opposite one another, as in, one is always up when the other is down, like a regular bike, to provide constant force while climbing, and the gearing system is linked to the rear wheel which individually provides propulsion. A road handcycle is very different in its setup. There is one wheel in the front and two wheels in the back, and the rider is laying supine almost entirely flat in a superbly aerodynamic position only a few inches from the ground. The pedals are symmetrical, meaning that both sides are in the same position at all times which provides increased balance. Turning is achieved through tilting of the front fork and the gears are linked to the front wheel which provides traction. I invite you to look up the different setups on YouTube as it can be challenging to explain but is easily understood when seen in action.

The first marathon I signed up to do was the Los Angeles marathon. My friend James Arnold, a very successful international corporate lawyer whom I had met through Facebook had invited me to stay in his penthouse in Marina Del Rey and had arranged for a VIP driver to take us anywhere we needed to go. While on the plane to Los Angeles, I had a very interesting encounter with the most puzzling flight attendant I had ever met. As I boarded the plane first which is customary for passengers requiring assistance and boarding with an aisle chair, she mentioned to the people helping me onto the plane to bring all other passengers with disabilities next to me in the same row regardless of their seat assignment because she liked it better when all the disabled people were grouped together. She asked me why I was going to Los Angeles and I responded that I was going to do the L.A. Marathon to which she quickly replied: "How about that?" almost rolling her eyes. There were two other people with various disabilities on the flight and we ended up seated next to one another. After we had landed and all the passengers had exited the plane, I was waiting for the helping crew to come get me with the aisle chair as it is also habitual that passengers requiring assistance deplane last. While I waited, the flight attendant came to ask me why I was still on the plane and if I thought I needed an aisle chair to exit. Did I think I needed an aisle chair? Let me think about this for a second. Two hours prior, I obviously couldn't move my legs and had to be wheeled in to my seat, but during the flight, half a cup of warm Pepsi and a small packet of magic peanuts had been bestowed upon me and maybe she knew something I didn't, and I was healed. I replied: "Let me try to move my legs." After staring at my knees for a couple of seconds with a flat face I looked back at her, smiled and added: "Yes, it looks like I'll need an aisle chair." She didn't think it was funny and immediately replied: "I don't know, you are the one who said you'll be doing the L.A. Marathon!" Then I understood that the concept of someone in a wheelchair doing a marathon can be confusing to people. Therefore, let me explain that there are, in general, several categories under which a marathon can be entered. There is obviously the usual category divided in men and women, and there is also a racing wheelchair category, and occasionally, albeit, much more rarely, a handcycle category.

I did not own a road handcycle but James had a friend in L.A. who was kind enough to let me borrow his for the event. The bike was not fitted to me at all, and was more of a casual bike than a racing bike and was in need of a serious tune-up, but it would suffice, and I was very grateful that it would allow me to participate. To be closer to the start of the marathon at Dodger Stadium, James had arranged for me to stay at the downtown Hilton the night before. Our trusty driver picked me up at 5am sharp. As we made our way to the stadium, the roads were gridlocked by the 23,628 participants equally trying to make their way to the starting line. Something amazing then happened! The driver started bypassing all the stopped vehicles by driving on the emergency lane. As we reached the parking lot of Dodger Stadium, the L.A.P.D. was trying to organize the mayhem of thousands of cars simultaneously dropping people off. My driver, wearing a black suit and tie over a crisp white shirt drove our massive black SUV straight to an officer, lowered his tinted window and said that he had a very important passenger in the back and needed to be allowed to go all the way to the front. I had never been labelled as "very important" before, and turned around to see if Robert Downey Jr. was sitting in the back row. As it happened, the officer allowed us through. Welcome to L.A.!

I was expediently dropped off at the starting line. While I had expected L.A. to be somewhat warm on that date of March 20th, 2011, it was actually unusually cold with temperatures in the low 40s. While waiting for the marathon to start, I realized that a bolt on the gearing mechanism was loose. Out of nowhere, a handcyclist from Mexico who was to my right, handed me a small Allen wrench saying: "Try this!" Like Cinderella's shoe, it was a perfect fit! I was blown-away. After tightening the bolt, I handed back the tool and the handcyclist told me to keep it as a souvenir. Sometimes, things happen in life that appear completely out of this world, because in fact, they are.

I wasn't too familiar with Los Angeles, aside from what I had seen on television and in movies, and during my short visit of Hollywood Boulevard years prior, but I was about to get a front line, high paced tour of the most iconic landmarks the city of angels had to offer. The horn was blown and the wheelchair racers and handcyclists, notoriously much faster as a group than any runner, were unleashed on the course first, like wild beasts. The energy was unbelievable as adrenaline was rushing through everybody's veins. Out of Dodger Stadium, we rode off on Vin Sully Avenue where already one of the racing wheelchairs crashed hard. It didn't take long to realize that the gearing mechanism was not functioning properly and I had to manually pick-up and lift the chain with bare fingers to move it from chainring to chainring to change gears. As a cohort, we then followed the motorcycle police escort onto Sunset Boulevard toward Chinatown. I was amazed that, in spite of the early morning hour, the course was densely lined with cheering supporters. I remember hitting the first serious hill at around mile 4, on West 1st Street, leading to the magnificent Disney Concert Hall. That hill considerably widened the gap between participants with the elite riders taking the lead. Once I reached the top of the hill at the corner of West 1st Street and North Grand Avenue, a supporter snapped a picture of me with my phone to immortalize the moment. It started raining and the cold rain fell harder and harder as we pushed against the frigid wind. My hands were frozen and my fingers were numb as a result, complicating the handling of the chain to change gears. I couldn't believe how insane the weather had become. Around mile 6 we reached Echo Park and at mile 10, reached the Hollywood Walk of Fame followed right after by Grauman's Chinese Theater. At mile 13 we were on Sunset Strip followed three miles later by Doheny Drive and Rodeo Drive in Beverly Hills. The Los Angeles Times reported that Beverly Hills had received 2 inches of rain, and water puddles were shin-deep in areas. It was a surreal experience to have hundreds of people lining the course, cheering us on as we went from famous landmark to famous landmark amidst the coldest and dampest conditions that could be expected in Southern California. At mile 18 we were on Santa Monica Boulevard, followed at mile 21 by Wilshire Boulevard. At mile 22 in Brentwood, NBC reported ankle-deep puddles of accumulated water. At mile 25, we entered Ocean Avenue and Palisades Park and finally reached the finish line by the Santa Monica Pier. As soon as I crossed the finish line at 2:34:11, I was wrapped in a thermal mylar safety blanket by volunteers to fend off hypothermia. Within minutes, James and our driver spotted me and whisked me into the

SUV and we quickly returned to the sauna room at the Azzurra condominiums in Marina Del Rey where I would slowly regain sensation in my hands.

The Los Angeles Times ran an article titled: "L.A. Marathon: Thousands evaluated for hypothermia." and NBC 4 ran an article titled: "L.A. Marathon: Record in the Rain." The L.A. Marathon was superbly organized and the course was extremely well marked. Despite the seriously harsh conditions, it was one of the most beautiful and memorable events I have ever been a part of, and it was a "breath-taking" experience both literally and figuratively.

CHAPTER 23

MARATHONS PART 1

Participation in sports for people with disabilities can be blindingly expensive and out of reach. While an able-body person needs a pair of tennis shoes and a racket to play tennis, a disabled person will need a racket and a $2,500 tennis wheelchair. For skiing, an able-body person needs boots, poles and skis and a disabled person needs one ski attached to a $5,500 sit-ski and $500 outriggers instead of poles. Similarly, to compete in marathons, an able-body person needs courage, determination, and a pair of running shoes while a disabled person needs courage, determination, and a $3,000 racing wheelchair or a $7,000 racing handcycle. I had plenty of courage and determination but was missing the apparatus. People often ask me why equipment adapted for use by people with disabilities is so expensive. The answer is simple: While mass production drives down the costs of items bought by many, the opposite is also true and items aimed at a very limited number of customers will have high production costs.

Wasatch Adaptive Sports had let me use all the equipment I had ever needed for downhill skiing, a recreational handcycle to routinely train around Liberty

Park and Sugarhouse Park in Salt Lake City and an off-road climbing handcycle to ride trails in the mountains. A friend had also let me borrow a tennis wheelchair. The only piece of equipment I had purchased was the adaptive cross-country ensemble which had set me back over $2,500.

The marathon in L.A. and my little stint in the Larry H. Miller Tour of Utah had made me fall in love with handcycling and I longed to participate in more venues. If I was to be competitive, I couldn't rely on the borrowing of recreational handcycles and needed my own racing equipment. I sold my cross-country rig and started saving money for a racing handcycle. Given the exorbitant prices of racing handcycles and my limited means on a resident's income, it quickly became evident that I would need some help. Many disabled athletes are able to secure grants for equipment through a wonderful organization called the Challenged Athlete Foundation. As with any charitable organization however, the funds are limited and while my income wasn't great, it was greater than that of others, since 40% of applicants declare annual incomes under $20,000. Of course, available grants should first go to those with the greatest financial need. I decided to look for used equipment which isn't easy considering the rarity of such specialized items. Realizing that elite athletes routinely update their equipment, I thought of contacting my Facebook friend, international Para triathlete Pierre Ouellet to see if he would consider selling me his old racing handcycle. Luckily, Pierre said that he had just received his new handcycle and could part with his old one. Even as a used handcycle, the price of this racing piece of equipment almost entirely made of carbon, amounted to more than I could afford. That's when my friend Steve Miller, President of the Larry H. Miller Tour of Utah and avid cyclist and philanthropist stepped in with a charitable donation to help me fill the gap so that I could purchase Pierre's handcycle and pursue my dream of training and competing. The handcycle was shipped from Quebec and arrived in Salt Lake City in a massive bike luggage. As I lacked storage space in my one-bedroom apartment, the beautiful handcycle found the perfect parking spot on top of the couch. In memory of Larry Miller, I wrote "RIDING FOR LARRY" on the bike, to remind myself to be as driven throughout my life as he had been throughout his.

TALLIX VON HAYDEN

Around the same time, after it had become evident that Elon would not be returned to me, I searched for another service dog, who would, as allowed by the Americans with Disabilities Act, be trained to be off-leash at all times. My friend Gail Miller with whom I frequently walked when I had Elon, had just acquired a German Shepherd bodyguard and I really liked the idea of a service dog that could double as personal protection since I was frequently by myself and could be seen as vulnerable by people with bad intentions. Because of this, I didn't look for a service dog in the usual places and instead, browsed websites dedicated to dogs trained for police work or personal protection. After diligent research, I adopted Tallix Von Hayden, a stunning black German Shepherd of impeccable pedigree and remarkable intelligence and aptitude. His handsome looks were very intimidating and instilled a combination of fear and admiration in anyone who met him for the first time. From the very moment I picked him up at the airport, we were inseparable. In fact, the only times we were ever apart were during marathons, until I purchased a dog trailer that was fitted behind the handcycle so that he could come with me anywhere, anytime.

My apartment building was renovating the gym and I was asked to make recommendations about the equipment. I recommended the acquisition of a Krankcycle which is a stationary arm bike that can be used by regular people as well as people in wheelchairs thanks to an easily removable seat allowing access from a wheelchair. While it was not feasible for me to routinely train directly on a handcycle, the krankcycle offered a convenient workout that closely mimicked the real activity. On the week-end, I would also push myself 3 miles up City Creek Canyon Road in my wheelchair, trying to reach the end of the asphalt road in less than 90 minutes. At the age of 36, I was asking a lot from my body in terms of physical activity, but it seemed to hold up well to the demand, so I kept pushing.

The handcycle did not fit in my car and I couldn't easily move it on my own, so I was dependent on Chris and Preston Langeland who were kind enough to accompany me to various marathons. Thanks to their help, I went on to complete the Salt Lake City Marathon on April 16th, 2011, followed by the Provo City Marathon on May 7th during which I secured a time of 1:35:59, cutting nearly an hour off my L.A. Marathon time. I continued with the Utah Valley Marathon on June 11th followed a month later by the Deseret News Marathon on July 25th.

The Salt Lake Marathon is big enough that traffic is well controlled and diverted but it isn't always the case in smaller venues. During the Provo City Marathon and the Utah Valley Marathon, I occasionally had to slow down or even stop at busy intersections along the course to ensure it was safe to proceed with crossing. The police standing guard at intersections is expecting slow runners at a certain time, not handcyclists reclined 2 inches off the road, buzzing through at significant velocities much sooner than anticipated. Having to slow down at intersections has a negative impact on the race because it always takes time to resume top speed after coming to a stop or slowing down.

A Record Finish

It was during the Deseret News Marathon that the stars lined up to allow me to deliver my best performance. Certainly, I had put a lot of work into my training and had improved both my power output and my endurance. I benefited from better equipment, and perhaps most importantly, the topography of the course and the favorable climate had a positive impact on my performance. In L.A. the weather had been horrendous with cold torrential rain, I competed on a poorly fitted borrowed handcycle in need of a tune-up on a course with a lot of uphill portions where all gear changes had to be done by lifting the chain with frozen fingers. In contrast, the Deseret News Marathon took place on a beautiful summer morning, on an incredibly light and aerodynamic, finely tuned, perfectly fitted carbon handcycle. The course incorporated two significant downhill portions down Big Mountain and Emigration Canyon and a motorcycle police escort led the way from start to finish, allowing me to blast through city intersections without worrying about surrounding traffic. That day, I achieved a personal and course record of 1:16:28, finishing the 26.2-mile course in less than half the time it had taken me to complete the L.A. Marathon just four months prior.

CHAPTER 24

MARATHONS PART 2

The next marathon on my list was the Top of Utah Marathon scheduled for September 17th in Logan, Utah, but first, Tallix and I had to pick someone up from the airport. I had stayed in touch with Sandra Gawehn, the German psychology student who had asked for permission to use my YouTube videos in her classes. We had corresponded with one another via email and had Skyped on a few occasions. One day, knowing that my marathon schedule would take me to Northern Utah and to a triple marathon around Lake Tahoe, I thought that it could be a beautiful vacation opportunity for her and invited her to come along if she wished. All she really knew about me was what transpired from my few YouTube videos, the fact that I was a physician, had climbed to Snowbird's summit, raced marathons with a handcycle, had my service dog taken away because of my lifestyle which was considered dangerous, and was living with an off-leash protection dog and a sweet little Dutch rabbit. Without hesitation, she agreed to hop on a plane to come meet me for a three-week vacation. In her mind, someone who lived with a free-roaming baby rabbit and a dog couldn't be all that bad.

Tallix and I picked up Sandra at the airport on September 15th which, coincidentally, was her 26th Birthday. The very next evening, after renting a minivan in which we all fitted, along with the handcycle, we drove up to Logan to check into our hotel. At the desk, the young woman told us that our room was on the 2nd floor with no elevator. Obviously, this represented a bit of an issue. She went on to explain that all other rooms had been booked and none were available. I pointed to the room with the handicap sign on the main floor and asked if it was also booked and she said that it was. I called Hotels.com and was informed that there was not a single available room in a 50-mile radius that night. I didn't know that the marathon in Logan was so popular. As we contemplated the options of either sleeping on the couch in the hotel's lobby, or in the minivan, the person who had been booked in the handicap accessible room came to check-in. He wasn't disabled and kindly agreed to trade rooms with me and take mine upstairs and the problem was solved. It was a good introduction to my life for Sandra who realized right away that nothing I do is ever easy or straightforward, and problems, or at least technical difficulties due to my being paralyzed, always seem to creep up from everywhere and have to be addressed.

The course of the Top of Utah Marathon was very difficult to follow. Upon reaching the bottom of Blacksmith Canyon Road where the course started, I continued straight, up a hill, which considerably slowed me down. Upon reaching the top of the hill, 500 yards later, a man who was parked to the side of the road asked me if I was part of the marathon and informed me that the course actually turned toward the city at the bottom of the hill, on South Hollow Road. I had just needlessly wasted valuable time climbing a hill that wasn't part of the course. Sometimes in life, we exert time and energy climbing hills that aren't ours to climb and those unnecessary detours could have been avoided with proper planning. There was no time to get upset, I turned around and rejoined the course, albeit with significant delay. For the life of me I couldn't figure out the turns that had to be made along the meandering course. I guesstimated my way toward the finish line in the Logan City Center and ended up on a parallel road, overshooting the course, and had to once again go back and rejoin the proper route. While all marathons are supposed to be 26.2 miles in length, I joke that this particular one, or at least the version I did, detours included, was closer to an even 28 miles.

Tahoe Triple

The following week-end, we returned to the rental agency to pick-up our minivan and they had forgotten to set-up the hand controls, so Sandra had to drive us all the way to Lake Tahoe for the Tahoe Triple Marathon. The Tahoe Triple Marathon was a back to back to back combination of the Emerald Bay Marathon on Friday September 23rd, 2011, the California Nevada Marathon on Saturday the 24th and the Lake Tahoe Marathon on Sunday the 25th. We stayed at Holly and Tim McGowan's house in Truckee, California. They had to go somewhere but before leaving, Tim had instructed us to make sure the doors were closed at night so bears wouldn't try to come inside. In the evening, we saw a deer looking through the kitchen window. Neither Sandra nor I were used to seeing this type of wildlife in the yard.

On the crack of dawn on Friday September 23rd, we met Les Wright, the organizer of the Tahoe Triple, on the southwest end of the lake for the start of the Emerald Bay Marathon that would take us from Inspiration Point just south of Emerald Bay in California to Spooner Summit in Nevada. Unlike any regular marathons that can be attended by hundreds, thousands or tens of thousands of people, less than one hundred "elite marathoners" and "ultramarathoners" showed up to do three marathons in a row. A few celebrities in the running world had shown up for the challenge, and among them was the renowned Blue Benadum, known as "Marathon Man" and whom I will talk about later. For the time being, suffice it to say that I took a look at his legs and was in awe at how muscular they were. Clearly this man was built for speed. I was, as was frequently the case, the sole handcyclist at the starting line. The organizer shot his gun in the air and off we were. The Emerald Bay Marathon started with a significant downhill portion, from 6,879 ft at inspiration point, to Lake level at 6,225 ft in about 4.5 miles, providing an excellent warm-up and allowing me to reach very high speeds only limited by a handful of tight turns at the top during which significant breaking had to occur. After going through a fairly dangerous stretch on unclosed roads in South Lake Tahoe, I crossed the Stateline between California and Nevada on U.S. Route 50 toward Zephyr Cove. About midway between Zephyr Cove and Glenbrook came the single most dangerous portion of the course: The crossing of Cave Rock Tunnel. About 300 ft before reaching the entrance of the tunnel is a special light warning system that informs drivers that a biker is in the dark tunnel. That light is activated by a button about 4.5 ft off the ground above a slightly slanted cement wall, entirely out of reach from my reclined position. Handcycles are so low to the ground, so wide because of the tricycle configuration and so rarely encountered in traffic, that drivers aren't used to looking out for them which can create very dangerous situations. The only option I had, aside from not entering the tunnel at all, was to accelerate as fast as I could during the 300 ft leading to the tunnel and continue to pedal for the 410 ft length of the tunnel as if my life depended on it, because it quite literally did. I never pedaled harder in my life! The last portion of the marathon was a gruesome climb from 6,360 ft around Glenbrook to the turn off toward Spooner Lake at around 7,000 ft in about 2.5 miles after having pedaled at full speed for 23.7 miles already. I gave it all I had and kept pushing forward when suddenly Blue passed me half way up the hill. I was bewildered as I hadn't been passed by a runner since the L.A. Marathon and never thought it would ever happen again. This guy was truly phenomenal! He climbed that hill, unphased, as if strolling through a park on a Sunday morning while I was spitting my lungs out. Upon finishing the marathon and after congratulating Blue on his mind-blowing performance, I waited in the sun for Sandra and Tallix to arrive in the minivan to pick me up. Without my wheelchair, I couldn't even get out of the handcycle and parked at the intersection of U.S. Route 50 and Nevada State Route 28 to wait. And indeed, I did wait for quite a while. Finally, I saw the minivan come down from Spooner Summit, from the direction of Carson City, which was the wrong way. Sandra had missed the left turn to NV-28 on the way up from Glenbrook and once she had realized the error, there was no way to turn around safely until reaching Carson City and coming back, which essentially represented a 30-mile round-trip detour.

Once reunited, we went to Sand Harbor Beach, hands-down one of the most beautiful places on the face of the earth. The weather could not have been better and we were the only car in the parking lot at this time of year and had the whole place to ourselves. After walking all the trails, we settled on the northernmost beach. In order to reach the water, I came down from my chair and into the sand and walked on my hands to the water while Sandra held my legs up. Sandra took beautiful pictures of Tallix and I, seated next to each other at the water's edge. It truly was a picturesque and memorable moment. It is a tradition for triple marathoners to cool off their legs in the lake after each marathon, and while my legs had not in the least contributed to the overall effort of covering the first 26.2-mile course, I sat in the crystal-clear water nonetheless.

The next morning, bright and early, we congregated at the starting line of the Cal-Neva Marathon at Spooner Summit. The Cal-Neva Marathon started with a 7.5 mile downhill with virtually no turns allowing me to reach record breaking speeds while dropping from 7,000 ft down to 6,225ft at the level of the Sand Harbor Beach State Park. After the sketchy event in the Cave Rock Tunnel the day before, I had Sandra follow me closely with the minivan to provide cover from the raging traffic. Upon reaching Incline Village, we cut left onto Lakeshore Boulevard and for the following three miles, rode through some of the most expensive real estate in the country before climbing to Crystal Bay at the Nevada-California Stateline. From Crystal Bay the course went downhill for the next 1.5 mile to King's Beach. Unfortunately for me, little climbs would come up here and there at a time when I was becoming quite exhausted. I was drinking a lot and eating sugar-rich gels to find the energy to maintain a relatively fast pace.

After Tahoe Vista was a climb around Flick Point before going down again toward Carnelian Bay. The durations of the downhill portions were so brief that they provided me with no rest. That being said, to be fair, whether on the downhill portions or the flats, it's not as if I was ever resting. I was flat-out all along, at all times, giving all my body could give. After covering 50 miles of Alpine terrain in 2 days, my body was begging me to stop. My level of exhaustion reached an all time high and I had to dig deep to muster the last iota of vigor I could give to climb the final hill around Dollar Point. After reaching the last apex, it was smooth sailing toward the finish line at Heritage Plaza in Tahoe City. Blue Benadum came shortly after and was the first runner through the finish line. We had a nice chat, took pictures, and he invited me to come run the Malibu International Marathon which he had created in his hometown. Unfortunately, because Malibu was a bit too long of a drive away, and because I didn't know how to travel with a handcycle in my luggage, I never was able to take him up on his offer and now regret to not have found a way to make it work.

    Sandra had parked the minivan on Grover Street next to the Tahoe Center of Natural Medicine and I can't think of a more picturesque place to practice the art of healing. We went down to the Tahoe City Marina and walked along the lakefront to Commons Beach. We then had a nice lunch prior to driving back to King's Beach and took a nice stroll along there as well. Sandra fell in love with Lake Tahoe the way I had fallen in love with this magnificent lake when I first saw it in the summer of 1995. I could write pages and pages about its natural beauty, but talented authors, from John Muir to Mark Twain have already celebrated this magical place more eloquently than

I ever could. I shall only add that Lake Tahoe should be on everybody's bucket list, as it is absolutely, without a doubt, a stunning destination that I wish everyone could see in their lifetime because it leaves an indelible positive mark on the soul.

    As demanding as the second marathon in the trilogy was, there was yet one last marathon to do. The third marathon for the triple marathon participants, but the main event for most single day marathoners was the Lake Tahoe Marathon. This event was the largest of the three in terms of the number of participants and is dubbed one of the most challenging marathons in the country. Prior to the start, all triple marathon participants came together for a group picture. I felt immensely proud to have pedaled my way into this small group of incredible athletes. All participants running the triple marathon and the single marathoners expected to run competitively and place on the podium were released first on the course. Naturally, being on a handcycle, I was first out the gate at Commons Beach in Tahoe City. Surprisingly, maybe because my body had given up complaining, I felt fresh and ready. The first half of the marathon was remarkably leveled, and I don't recall having to battle any major hill on the way to Homewood and Tahoma on California Route 89. The course curved around Meeks Bay and then on to Emerald Bay. The way to the Emerald Bay State Park is a gradual climb, but one particular section called "Hell's Hill" was marked with funny signs such as "Welcome to Hell's Hill", "6,600' Purgatory" and "100' Heaven." After looping around Emerald Bay and admiring its breathtaking vistas it was downhill again toward Camp Richardson and the finish line on Pope's Beach near South Lake Tahoe, where I collected my third medal in three days. Blue Benadum, once again, was the first runner to come through the finish line.

Blue is a phenom and a celebrated athlete having completed 60 marathons in a ten-year period between 26 and 36 years of age. He is the founder of the Los Angeles Speed Project comprising L.A.'s most talented distance runners. Blue finished the Emerald Bay Marathon in 2:48:25, the Cal-Neva Marathon in 2:48:27 and the Lake Tahoe Marathon in 2:57:22. His total time over the three events was 8:38:39 which, considering the elevation, the multiple climbs, but also the downhills which can be almost as punishing on the legs, is nothing short of amazing. It was an honor and a privilege for me to participate in this triple marathon alongside such a decorated runner.

CHAPTER 25

LAS VEGAS

Before departing from Truckee to return to Salt Lake City after the Triple Marathon, as we were chatting with Tim McGowan, he mentioned that the way back was easy, we just had to go 80 all the way. About 2 and a half hours later, as we were working our way East on I-80, at 80mph, I spotted a Nevada Highway patrol car on the median in the distance. There weren't many cars on the road and as soon as we passed him, he turned on his lights and came after us. We pulled over and waited for the patrolman to walk toward us. I lowered my window and upon being asked why we were being stopped, I explained that we were driving back from Lake Tahoe on our way to Salt Lake City and that our friend had told us to drive 80 all the way. As I said it out loud, I realized that he meant I-80 and not 80mph. The patrolman, after learning that we were German and French went on a tirade about Germans and how the portion of I-80 crossing Nevada wasn't the Autobahn. He also explained that other Germans had left the country before paying their speeding ticket and had been arrested during their next visit to the U.S. He told us that according to the law in Nevada, if the speed limit is 75mph, then any speed above 75 would get us a ticket as he had zero tolerance for speeding. He went on and on and on. He was making fair points and we had no objection. Suddenly, the patrolman spotted Tallix on the back seat. He asked what kind of dog he was, and I explained that he was a black German Shepherd. Right away his demeanor changed and he mentioned that he also had a German Shepherd in his patrol car as he was part of a K9 unit. He asked us to sit tight as he went back to his car and returned with a "Nevada Highway Patrol K9 Unit" sticker that he gave us as a gift. After complementing Tallix on his handsome looks, he gave us a verbal warning and told us to slow down to the speed limit and be safe on the way back to Utah. We learned a good lesson: Contrary to popular belief, "5 over" isn't ok in the state of Nevada.

For the remainder of Sandra's vacation, we drove to Bryce Canyon, and then to Las Vegas. While driving south on I-15 from Salt Lake City, I was so focused on the conversation Sandra and I were having that I forgot to check the gas gauge. When I checked the gauge, some 160 miles south of Salt Lake City, the dashboard indicated that I had 0 mile left before running out of gas. Fortunately, right then, I spotted a sign on the side of the freeway stating that the nearest exit for gas was 1.5 mile away. Half a mile later, another sign indicated Exit 146, Kanosh 1 Mile. Things were looking good. As we neared the exit, we realized there was no gas station right at the exit as is usually the case. We had to drive to town to find the gas station, but had no idea how far we had to drive to get there. We only knew that we were in the middle of nowhere, without gas. After driving under I-15, we proceeded to drive north toward Kanosh, population 487. As soon as we got onto the road to Kanosh it became obvious that it was a longer stretch than we had hoped, as in, dangerously long when already driving on the reserve. Half way down the road, about 3 miles in, the car stuttered, coughed and came to a halt. I pulled to the side of the road and got out planning to walk the rest of the way to go get gas. After getting out and rolling 3 ft in my wheelchair, the palms of my hands got stabbed by razor sharps thorns. There were thumbtack-like little balls with multiple thorns each, all over my tires and my hands, that we learned later, are Tribulus Terrestris, colloquially known in the Utah desert as Goat's Heads. Poor Tallix had them in his paws as well. Within a minute, my palms were red, swollen and irritated. We were not looking good as we embarked on the 8-mile round trip hike to Kanosh to get gas. Fortunately, a huge truck pulling a very long horse trailer came driving toward us. The driver offered to drive into town to get enough gas for us so that we could drive to the gas station on our own. I was delighted. When the truck came back, the three occupants got out wearing full cowboy gear, including hat, boots, and leather chaps. Sandra had never seen that outfit in real life. It was like seeing John Wayne in the flesh. We were very grateful for their assistance. After her experience of getting pulled over by a highway patrolman in Nevada, Sandra was able to add "Rescued by genuine cowboys in the Utah desert" to the list of activities she had participated in during her American vacation. We got back in the car and drove into town where we pulled into a gas station that was straight out of a movie, with three old men wearing blue jean overalls sat on a bench outside. It was a strangely picturesque experience for us to get gas in Kanosh. Sometimes, little hiccups happen in life to allow us to experience things we might have never experienced otherwise and broaden our minds in the process. As unfortunate as running out of gas in the desert seemed at the time, I now cherish this memory dearly because I know that every time I am the recipient of someone's kindness I become a better person as the experience softens my soul and strengthens my hope in humanity.

We worked our way down to Bryce Canyon, one of my favorite places on the face of the earth. Sandra had never seen such breathtaking landscapes of ochre-colored gravity-defying rock formations. She enjoyed the scenery as much as I did and I was glad to share this experience with her. Finally, we traveled to Las Vegas and stayed at the Trump Hotel because it is smoke-free and doesn't have a Casino. While it was the first week-end in October, the weather was very hot. After walking from the Trump Hotel to the south end of the strip and back up to the level of the Bellagio, we tried to hail a cab for the way back to the hotel. A lot of people were waiting in line, and a lot of taxis were also waiting in their own line. As Sandra, Tallix and I reached the front of the line, the first taxi refused to take us and simply drove past us. This had happened to me before as some taxi drivers don't want to have to deal with the wheelchair. When I traveled to Los Angeles right after my accident, the first two taxis in the airport line refused to take me until the LAX police forced the third taxi to take me. He was so upset that, after taking the wheels off, he just put the wheelchair frame on my lap to make sure I would be as bothered as he was. In Paris, a taxi had refused to take me as well stating that the wheelchair was an issue. This time, we were in front of the Bellagio, tired, hot, and eager to find our way back to the hotel. The second taxi also drove by, signaling that he didn't want to take us. The third taxi driver pointed to Tallix and lowered his window to explain that he'd rather miss his turn and drive back to the end of the line than to take us. The crowd of intoxicated people behind us was getting agitated by the fact that we were holding up the line so we decided to walk back to the hotel. Sandra asked me if there were protective laws against such discrimination. I explained that there were very strict protective laws but that unfortunately, there was an occasional discrepancy between the laws and their application in the real world.

We had a great week-end nonetheless and Sandra had a tremendously entertaining three-week vacation. She and I had traveled a fair amount together, had gotten along very well and had fallen in love. I realized that in life, the happy moments were amplified, and the challenges were attenuated when those were shared with a loved one rather than experienced alone. I asked Sandra if she would want to be my co-pilot through the rest of our lives and she said yes. Just like that, we were engaged the evening before she flew back to Germany. In her first three weeks in the U.S., we had gotten stopped for going 5 miles an hour over the speed limit in Winnemucca, we had ran out of gas in Kanosh and been rescued by cowboys and we had gotten engaged. Clearly, this looked like a good start for what would become an epic journey together.

My final marathon of the year was back in Las Vegas on December 4th. Chris Langeland was kind enough to drive Tallix and me. I learned at the starting line that handcycles were not allowed, and that only racing wheelchairs could participate. Because we had traveled quite a long distance to get there, after begging the organizers to allow me to participate, they agreed to let me enter the race with the caveat that it would be an unofficial entry and that my time wouldn't be counted. It didn't bother me, I was once again happy just to be part of the experience. The event, starting in the evening, was very well organized with excellent police support and the roads were beautifully blocked for the safety of the participants.

Racing at night on the Las Vegas Strip was another experience that was added to my bank of cherished memories.

A Cracking Revelation

After completing a total of eleven marathons, I underwent a CT of the thoracic spine during a routine follow-up with my neurosurgeon. The imaging study revealed that, the fall I had suffered off my chair while tangled in a t-shirt almost a year before, had caused a compression fracture of the T5 vertebra. While I had erroneously thought, at the time, that my cervical spine could have been affected, we realized that in fact, it was the vertebra right above the spinal fusion where all the compressive forces were concentrated that had taken the bulk of the impact and had fractured. At that point, months after the accident, the fracture had healed and there was no indication for surgery. At least the vertebral fracture provided an explanation for the discomfort I had experienced in my back while laying flat at night, or while reclined in my handcycle while completing eleven marathons in a twelve-month period.

Did You Win?

Before I conclude the chapters pertaining to marathons, I would like to offer an observation. Frequently, after a marathon, people asked me if I won. While a fair question, it focuses too much on the act of winning and not enough on the value of participation which

I think is a mistake. Out of over 26,000 participants in the L.A. Marathon for example, there is technically only one individual crossing the finish line first, and yet the beauty about marathons, which is also coincidentally the beauty in life, is that everyone getting to the finish line is a winner for having endured to the end. Ernest Hemingway said: "There is nothing noble in being superior to your fellow man; True nobility is being superior to your former self." In the same spirit, my goal in participating in marathons was never to be better than anyone else, but rather, to be better than my prior self by training for and achieving a goal I had set for myself. Marathon results tend to be broken down in a few categories, but I take that fractionating process further and consider that everyone is participating in a category of their own and their participation alone lives on its own merit, and is a victory in itself. Some people can finish a marathon in a smudge over two hours while others may need five hours to complete the task. Both accomplishments, while different, are commendable. The former is commendable for the speed at which the goal was accomplished, and the latter, for the sustained effort it required to reach the goal over a longer period of time. Both accomplishments have inherent merit for what they represent. Everybody is different and people should fight their own battles, run their own race and pursue their own dreams. I always urge people interested in participating in a marathon to not worry about the pace of others and only focus on the race against their own self. That advice stands true for life in general. Too often people worry about what others are doing when their efforts would be better focused on doing the best they can in their own life. In a marathon, as in life, coming first is overrated and participation is most important because the accomplishment of a worthy goal that requires continued effort makes everyone a winner, no matter the pace.

Ethelbert Talbot, an American Episcopalian Bishop is credited for having inspired Pierre de Coubertin to formulate the Olympic creed during a speech given to the Olympic champions at the 1908 London Summer Olympic Games. The Olympic creed is as follows: "The most important thing in the Olympic Games is not to win but to take part, just as the most important thing in life is not the triumph but the struggle. The essential thing is not to have conquered but to have fought well."

CHAPTER 26

MULTIPLE SCLEROSIS FELLOWSHIP

As I neared the end of my residency training in Physical Medicine and Rehabilitation (PM&R), I contemplated pursuing a fellowship training and asked Brooks Rohlen who, at the time, was doing a fellowship at Stanford University, for his opinion. His response was clear: "It's a no-brainer. You didn't study all your life to stop so close to the finish line." It was inconceivable to him to cap off so many years of studies without a fellowship, the highest possible post-doctoral educational level attainable in the United States educational system.

I initially looked at what many people considered the obvious route: A fellowship in Spinal Cord Injury Medicine and contacted the directors at the combined program of Stanford University and the Palo Alto VA Medical Center. However, the more I thought of it, the more I realized that perhaps, focusing on the treatment and management of a condition I myself had, could set me up for some peculiar challenges that I may not have been prepared to handle so early in my career. While building a rapport with patients was easy, creating an acceptable professional barrier between patient and physician was much harder when both had a similar condition. From my experience in residency, spinal cord injured patients were understandably curious and interested in how I personally handled this, that or the other. There was no professional barrier whatsoever and all questions seemed fair game. If I explained the way to manage a particular issue in general terms, the ensuing question was inevitably: "How do you do it?"

Having been the recipient of much financial support from Ann and Mitt Romney while I was going through residency, I was emotionally deeply indebted to them and was eagerly looking for a way to pay their kindness forward. Because they had been very involved in supporting Multiple Sclerosis research, I knew the fight against this neurological condition was dear to them. Perhaps I could dedicate a portion of my career as a physician to care for patients with Multiple Sclerosis (MS). The PM&R training I had acquired through residency had provided me with a solid base on how to address some of the symptoms affecting patients with MS, but I had yet to learn everything else about this complicated neurological condition. Dr. Monica Rojas, my neighbor and friend was working in Dr. John W. Rose's neuroimmunology research lab at the VA Medical Center at the time, and after discussing my thoughts with her, she proposed to set up a meeting with Dr. Rose who had trained fellows in the past, whom had subsequently become leaders in the field at several of the most prestigious institutions in the country. Dr. Rose is a giant in the field of neuroimmunology and is a very prolific researcher, who, to date, has published 167 papers. To my greatest delight, he agreed to take me on as a clinical fellow and together, we applied for funds from the National Multiple Sclerosis Society to fund my fellowship at the University of Utah. I became one of only thirteen MS fellows in the country that year, and only one of two physiatrists as the majority of the fellows were neurologists by training.

While my fellowship was only a little over a year, it was a tremendously productive time during which I learned a lot. The topic of Multiple Sclerosis was fascinating to me and as I learned new things, I presented my newly acquired knowledge to the staff of the neuroimmunology lab at the VA at a weekly conference over lunch on Fridays. The atmosphere of those lectures in a small group, among friends, was less intimidating than actual Grand Rounds. During my residency training I had given three Grand Rounds for the PM&R Department respectively titled: "The Politics of Stem Cells", "Service Dogs for People with Disabilities" and "Eponyms: The Stories behind the Names." Each time was a tense experience that I dreaded because Grand Rounds are scrutinized, judged and scored, and I was so nervous that my delivery was fair at best. During my fellowship however, I received valuable coaching from my mentor and developed skills as a speaker through repeated practice in a not only non-threatening, but an encouraging environment. I learned through experience that confidence comes from mastering the topic at hand. Throughout the year, I was asked to speak about MS for the Utah Caregiver Coalition, the lecture series on Improving Quality of Life in MS, the Healthcare in Leadership Continuing Education for the Society for Social Work, the MS Research Conference at the Brain Institute at the University of Utah and the VISN 19 Pharmacy Conference for the University of Wisconsin-Madison. Additionally, while continuing to lecture once yearly to the medical students on the topic of spinal cord injury, I also regularly lectured to the medical students and the neurology residents about multiple sclerosis.

Having been encouraged by the approval for publication of the article I had written about intersection syndrome in a handcyclist in the journal Topics of Spinal Cord Injury Rehabilitation, I decided to pick another topic pertaining to MS that I could study in its most intricate details and submit my findings for publication. After having lectured frequently on the topic of bladder management in MS, I wrote an article titled: "Advances in the Management of Neurogenic Detrusor Overactivity in Multiple Sclerosis" which was published in the International Journal of MS Care.

During my fellowship, being interested in the cost of pharmacotherapies in general, I carefully studied the cost of medications used in the management of various MS symptoms. This interest culminated in two research posters about the "Pharmacoeconomics of Multiple Sclerosis" that were presented at the 2011 Tykeson Fellows Conference in Dallas and the 2012 Paralyzed Veterans of America Summit in Las Vegas.

Benefitting from the tutelage of Dr. John W. Rose and his clinical team, especially Julia Klein, and Dr. Dana DeWitt, I flourished into a proficient lecturer and budding expert on the topic of multiple sclerosis. Toward the end of the year, I delivered a Grand Rounds lecture for the Department of Neurology on the topic of Bladder Management in MS.

A Dog Lover's Meeting Place

The MS clinic, located in the Imaging and Neurosciences Center in Research Park at the University of Utah was the perfect location for Tallix because the massive patch of grass between the clinic and This is The Place Heritage Park was the official meeting place for a lot of dog lovers. Dog owners would gather in the afternoon and evening to walk a loop together with their dogs and watch the sunset over the Great Salt Lake as a group. Tallix and I made a lot of friends and we enjoyed spending time outside playing catch with other dogs after work. Tallix was a fierce competitor and ran after tennis balls for hours, sometimes until complete exhaustion. He was so powerful that big patches of grass would come flying off his paws when he started running and while balls were thrown at respectable distances with a "Chuckit ball launcher" Tallix frequently caught them mid-air before they could bounce. His five Labrador friends gave a good effort but didn't stand a chance.

Underserved Area Service Mandate

I loved the environment and the people I worked with at the University of Utah and would have been very pleased to stay in Salt Lake City after my fellowship. That being said, I was reminded of the fact that I was still French, and while I had been granted a visa to pursue my post-doctoral training, I would need to be sponsored for a green card in order to stay in the United States. Employers petition for green cards for foreign workers who could perform a function when local American workers aren't available to fulfill the particular job. Consequently, popular areas such as Salt Lake City with a growing population and tremendous influx of people from other states aren't favored when it comes to the distribution of green cards because there is plenty of local talent. Rural areas that may have a difficult time recruiting skilled talent in specific industries simply have a greater need when it comes to the allocation of green cards. Therefore, in order to get a green card, I needed to fill a position in an underserved area, which requirement would most likely take me out of Utah.

I got in touch with a nationwide physician recruiter and explained the situation with which he was very familiar, having worked with a high number of foreign physicians before. Essentially, he broke it down as follows: "You have three choices, Nebraska, Iowa or Oklahoma." I knew very little about these states, so Sandra and I went on the internet for a crash course on the Midwest and the South-Central region.

I had learned that Iowa was in need of MS specialists during a conference with the National MS Society, so Iowa was definitely a place where I wanted to interview. The recruiter lined-up interviews in both Nebraska and Iowa. My first interview was in Lincoln, Nebraska at an excellent rehabilitation hospital. The state-of-the-art facility was second to none, boasted high-tech rehabilitative equipment I had never seen before and was genuinely impressive. My second interview was in Waterloo, Iowa at another, brand new, albeit smaller rehabilitation facility that offered great potential for the development of an MS Clinic. Truly, it must be said that the people were lovely at both facilities Tallix and I visited. Ultimately, when it came time to decide where to go, I opted for what subjectively appeared to be the most dog-friendly environment because Tallix and I came as an inseparable unit. In Waterloo, the physician recruiter from the hospital had asked a lot of questions to ensure that Tallix was comfortable during our visit and had included dog treats in the gift basket which was a small but very meaningful gesture. Also, my prospective partner and her husband were absolute dog lovers so we would be in great company. I decided to sign my first contract out of training with Wheaton Franciscan Healthcare to work at Covenant Hospital in Waterloo, Iowa and was very optimistic about what the future had in store for us.

CHAPTER 27

WATERLOO PART 1

During my second trip to Waterloo for a pre-employment onboarding meeting and to look for a home, Tallix and I were being flown in First Class. We were on the front row which was fantastic since Tallix had plenty of room to lay at my feet. It was my first time flying First Class and I was looking forward to a comfortable flight when the man seated to our left called the flight attendant. When she asked him what he needed he responded: "I did not pay for a First Class ticket to be seated next to a dog." The flight attendant didn't know how to respond and offered him free miles for his inconvenience. He replied: "I don't need your miles, I just wanted to make a point." On that note, I leaned toward him and whispered: "The only point you made is that my dog is more of a gentleman than you are."

As the realtor took me on a tour of the city, I was amazed that whenever we saw people in their yard while driving by, they waved and smiled. I asked if she knew the people and she replied that she didn't. I asked why everybody waved at us and she said that they were just saying hello. I was immediately charmed by the Midwest hospitality.

I had used the internet to preview a few houses for sale in Waterloo, located within a ten-minute drive of the hospital. The real estate prices in Waterloo were about a fourth of what similar homes would fetch in Salt Lake City so essentially, everything looked very cheap to me. We drove through a neighborhood called Prospect which looked very much like the Federal Heights neighborhood in Salt Lake City or any upscale residential neighborhood in America. Not far from Prospect was a beautiful property, standing like an island on an isolated triangular lot with no adjacent neighbors as it was surrounded by three different streets. The home, erected in 1919 stood like a Grande Dame on a hill. I never thought I could possibly own such a magnificent property. Over the years, it had been the home of influential members of the community and rumor has it that Richard Nixon had lunch there while campaigning in Iowa for the Presidency of the United States in the 1960s. Most recently, it had been the home of a couple of wealthy interior designers who had significantly upgraded its look, followed by a surgeon in otolaryngology who had owned it for many years and had kept it in great shape, followed by the then current owner, a general surgeon who had also made some valuable upgrades to the property. It was love at first sight. Not only the house was beautiful, it was also relatively inexpensive in the Iowa market. Clearly, as the realtor pointed out, with a grand staircase in the front entrance, a split-level entry in the back and four floors in total, the house was not exactly wheelchair accessible. She was absolutely correct. If someone had purposefully designed a non-accessible home, they might have come up with the floorplan of that house. I went in, dropped down from my chair onto the ground and crawled up the stairs to the main floor and up the main staircase to what is technically the third floor where the master bedroom and ensuite bathroom were located. The ceiling of the marble bathroom was domed and painted like the sky. The only place I had ever seen anything like it was at the Caesars Palace in Las Vegas. Certainly, that house was impractical to say the least but all I could think of, was how proud my parents would be if I owned such an imposing piece of real estate. I devised to have a stair glider built between the first three floors and signed the paperwork to purchase the home later that day. As it turned out, the cost of the custom-made stair glider rail was much greater than the television advert had led me to believe, and I was only able to afford the connection between the basement and the main floor with my signing bonus. The stair glider to the bedrooms would have to wait.

Sandra, who could only visit less than three months at a time, and a total of less than six months a year on a tourist visa, planned to be with Edonis, Tallix and I during our move. We had my car shipped while we flew to Cedar Rapids Airport. I held Edonis on my lap in her carry-on travel box while Tallix laid at our feet.

Upon arriving at the airport, I noticed that the Iowa flag was essentially a French flag with a bald eagle holding a ribbon in the center, under which is written IOWA. The ribbon is inscribed with the following: "Our liberties we prize and our rights we will maintain." The blue, white and red was meant to reflect Iowa's history as part of the French Louisiana Territory. Designed in 1917, it was adopted as the Iowa Flag in 1921, interestingly, two years after our house was built.

The stair glider leading from the basement to the main floor was installed quickly. The basement became the master bedroom but also had a bathroom, walk-in closet, laundry room, wood workshop and an area previously used as a sauna with a hot tub that I converted into a gym. As a design detail, the laundry room had a single step down and the bathroom had a single step up rendering those two rooms inaccessible to me in the wheelchair. Marek Rozek, husband to my partner Dr. Barbara Rozek was one of the kindest, hardest working person I have ever met. In addition to being a valuable Physician Assistant in the Neurosurgery Department, he also provided care in the Emergency Department. He happened to be very handy and a brilliant wood worker and when he saw the steps in the basement and the accessibility issues those represented, he took it upon himself to remedy the situation. He went to Menards, a large home improvement store prevalent in the Midwest, to get the supplies he would need to build a ramp in the bathroom and a full floating floor in the laundry room. He worked tirelessly late into the evening for several days before the task was accomplished and always refused any type of payment for his time or the supplies that he used. He did it all out of the goodness of his heart. He and his wife were outstanding human beings and I felt fortunate to work with them every day. Tallix was an amazing judge of character and loved them both dearly.

The hospital where I worked had undergone serious renovation efforts and was very nice. The entire rehabilitation floor, the rehabilitation clinic and our offices were all brand new. Before I had come, my partner, Dr. Malicka Rozek had told me that it was a pleasure for her to come in to work in the morning, and after having worked there a little, I absolutely concurred. The administrators were very supportive of anything I was interested in pursuing and I had the opportunity to attend TOXINS 2012, the conference of the International Neurotoxin

Association, held at the Eden Roc in Miami Beach, within the first two months of starting work. While the general population is familiar with botulinum toxin with regard to its cosmetic application, it has a wide variety of other uses, including the management of excessive underarm sweating, the management of muscle spasms, the management of overactive urinary bladder and the prevention of chronic headaches. In the field of rehabilitation pertaining to the care of patients with strokes, cerebral palsy, spinal cord injuries or multiple sclerosis, the primary use is the control of muscle spasticity and increasingly, the control of overactive bladder which is delegated to our urology partners to whom we refer patients. The conference covered all possible applications and offered valuable practical training. As a benefit of my attendance I was able to add the prevention of chronic headaches via the use of botulinum toxin as a service to the community.

The marketing team of the hospital did a fabulous job announcing my presence in the area and introducing to the community the services that I could provide. One day, out of the blue, while driving to Menards in the evening, I looked up to an illuminated electronic billboard to see my picture, in a white coat. The billboard announced me as "The Region's only Fellowship trained MS specialist." Tallix and I ended up in the local paper as well as on television several times and I gave occasional radio interviews. While the purpose of the exposure was to promote my medical services to the community, Tallix was such a stunningly beautiful animal that he always stole the show, becoming the star of every featured appearances. One article published in the Waterloo-Cedar Falls Courier was titled: "Covenant doctor gets by with a little help from man's best friend." The article stated how Tallix had quickly made a name for himself in the cedar valley. Through placards with his picture at all entrances and all elevators of Covenant Medical Center, and through pictures in the newspaper and television appearances, Tallix became an instant celebrity. Every time we got out of the house to go grocery shopping, go to the home improvement store or go on walks, it wouldn't take long before someone would recognize him and approach me to ask if he was Tallix, Covenant's dog. It was a really nice way to meet people.

MS Clinic

Covenant Medical Center was very helpful in launching my MS career, and thanks to the help of several local neurologists referring patients with MS to my care, I was quickly able to grow the MS clinic. During my first year at Covenant, I was asked to work for several pharmaceutical compagnies as a consultant and lecturer. In that capacity, Tallix and I spent most of our vacation time from the hospital essentially touring the country, lecturing and educating neurologists and patients about the intricacies of multiple sclerosis. In the clinic setting, while necessary, it can be difficult to find the time to explain MS in detail. These speaking engagements provided valuable opportunities to explain what MS was to very large groups consisting of sometimes more than 400 people at a time. This chronic autoimmune disease can be easy to explain in its basic form but the wide array of symptoms it can cause and the many different shapes that its course can take quickly complicate the discussion. Furthermore, the multiple pharmacologic agents used in its treatment have different mechanisms of action which can be incredibly difficult to grasp for people who aren't experts in neuroimmunology. With practice, remembering the value of the art of simplification that I first experienced from Dr. William D. Phillips, I was able to explain complex concepts in a manner that could be understood by almost every audience. I made use of illustrations and metaphors and drew parallels with ideas with which the audience was familiar, to enable people to understand how the various medications worked, and what made them different from one another. I thoroughly enjoyed this part of my professional activity and frequently stated that if I could do only one thing, lecturing about MS would be my activity of choice because it enabled me to reach so many people and improve their understanding of the condition that afflicted them. In a three-year period, Tallix and I traveled all over the country and boarded upwards of 200 flights. Tallix was never on a leash, always leading the way through the airport. I used to click my tongue so he could hear me following him as we speedily cruised through busy airports. When we deplaned, always coming out of the gate last, occasionally, groups of oncoming passengers would crowd the exit, especially at Chicago O'Hare and Tallix made sure to come out first and split the crowd the way Moses split the Red Sea so that I could pass through. It only took a couple of menacing barks to make people move swiftly out of the way. By the time I emerged from the gate, there was a nice wide path through the crowd and many people had their cameras out to take pictures and videos of Tallix in action. Seeing Tallix work the crowd at a busy airport was truly a beautiful event to behold. Nothing intimidated him. We frequently benefitted from courtesy upgrades to First Class where Tallix would be assigned his own seat. Also, because the travels were professionally organized, drivers were assigned to pick us up to take us anywhere we needed to go so that we never had to bother with regular taxis, which, as I explained before can sometimes be a problem.

On one occasion I had been booked to give a lecture at the Westin Kierland Resort in Scottsdale. Coincidentally, Vice President Joe Biden was staying in the same hotel. As members of the Secret Service carried out inspections through the hotel with the assistance of their own leashed black German Shepherds, one of their young dogs came a bit too close to me for Tallix's taste and he quickly body-checked him away from me. Tallix had a good 30lbs on the other dog who offered no resistance and immediately understood his place in the pecking order. The Secret Service dog handler remarked that he had never seen a civilian dog overpower his own dog before. Tallix wasn't just any civilian dog. At home, on the rare occasions that people dared coming to knock at the back door, he would stand against the door, look out the window and bark in a way that would make anyone fear for their life. If I asked him to "Protect" he would go into full attack mode and launch his 110lb frame toward any intruder at blistering speeds, but at the same time, would stop on a dime if asked to do so and was very docile toward patients and staff members in the hospital. I have walked at night in Chicago, San Francisco, Saint Louis and never once felt endangered with him at my side.

We were fortunate to have our dear neighbors and friends Kathy and Bob Elgas volunteer to watch after Edonis when Tallix and I were traveling. Kathy would come feed her twice a day and spend time playing with her so that she wouldn't be bored.

CHAPTER 28

WATERLOO PART 2

Waterloo is routinely ranked among the top 25 coldest cities in America. As soon as we moved in, people mentioned how brutally cold Iowa winters could be. Naively, I had thought that after spending a good chunk of time in the Wasatch front in Utah, I was prepared for a cold environment. I was wrong. January 2014 boasted record low temperatures amidst a polar vortex. I loosely remember that temperatures did not rise above freezing for over five continuous weeks and in fact, remained well below freezing most of the time. One week in February, as we were driving to the airport on our way to Miami for a conference, the temperature gauge on my car read -25 F (-32 C) which was a fairly common occurrence. On our way back, on the flight from Miami to Chicago O'Hare, we flew over the southern tip of lake Michigan and saw that it was a solid block of ice from shore to shore.

When asked how cold it is in Iowa, I try to explain that it so cold that it actually makes it difficult to breathe. Sandra has experienced this as well. It is as if, midway through the first breath, breathing stops as the body isn't keen on taking in such frigid air. The key is to breathe slowly, preferably through a scarf, and through the nose to allow the air to slightly warm up in the nasal turbinates before entering the lungs. Of course, it goes without saying that wearing protective clothing is imperative in the prevention of frostbite which can occur in a very short amount of time.

As temperatures warmed up, we experienced freezing rain, which I had never seen before. Freezing rain is when actual water droplets are falling through the atmosphere but instantly turn into ice upon contacting cold surfaces. This created a singular sheet of thick ice across the entire driveway on which even Tallix could not walk on his way to the yard. We purchased very large outdoor rubber mats that we lined up over the ice to make a path so that Tallix could go out and do his business.

The weather remained cold well into the spring, but not cold enough to prevent us from taking long walks around the neighborhood. On harsh days, we would only walk around Columbus Circle, a mere 0.6-mile loop, but on good days, we would walk all over the place until the GPS on my phone indicated that we had covered 3 miles.

The home was located a short walking distance away from a large park with a golf course, a pool and sixteen beautifully maintained tennis courts open to the public, free of charge. As I was able to purchase my own tennis chair and had tennis courts readily available, Sandra and I started playing tennis quite regularly after work. Eventually I developed lateral epicondylitis commonly known as tennis elbow. I relied on my arms so much that complete rest was not feasible, thus delaying the healing process. For the first six months, the pain was so severe that I couldn't open a door using a spherical knob. Overall,

I suffered significant pain for nearly a year and was forced to completely stop playing tennis for that entire period.

Jack and Marna Creery, our lovely neighbors from across the street, introduced me to the complex network of bike trails the city had to offer and we went on bike rides, them on their bikes and me on my handcycle, pulling a trailer with Tallix. That activity didn't seem to hurt and gave me the opportunity to visit new places.

I continued lifting quite heavy weights on a regular basis, doing 100 reps of bench presses with 50lbs free weights in each hand, but my right shoulder was showing signs of failure, constantly grinding and clicking with overhead movements. One day, as I was climbing the stairs on my hands while Sandra held my legs to get onto our upper deck, I felt an intense pain deep into the right shoulder. The pain was such that it instantly brought tears to my eyes. I had torn the labrum. I received a corticosteroid injection which did almost nothing to relieve the pain. It took many months for me to recover, albeit incompletely, from this injury. Little by little, my upper body upon which I was heavily relying, was slowly starting to give out. Getting in and out of the handcycle became more and more difficult. Playing tennis was entirely out of the question, as was lifting weights. Suddenly, I found myself pulling on light therapeutic elastic bands attached to a door handle as a form of exercise, simply to recover basic function.

CHAPTER 29

WATERLOO PART 3

The reason why a position had opened up for me in Waterloo in the first place was because the physician who was filling it before me had decided to join the military and provide rehabilitative care to injured soldiers at Walter Reed Hospital in Washington DC. He was initially anticipating retiring after his stint in the military. After about a year and a half, he changed his mind and decided to come back to Waterloo, which created a somewhat difficult situation given that I was now occupying the position the hospital had to give back to him because he had been serving his country during his absence. Because they wouldn't consider letting me go in order to reabsorb him into the staff, we ended up with three physicians doing what two physicians could do, which left me with a lot of free time. I couldn't complain to have reduced work hours, but worried about the impact this slowed-down pace could have on my career which was in its infant stage. The power of inertia can be powerful, and I didn't want to be at rest so early in my career.

During my third year in Waterloo, while the administration was incredibly supportive of the new structure and willing to keep me on staff no matter what, I became uncertain about my future at Covenant Medical Center. Around the same time, I started receiving phone calls from very prominent figures in the MS world such as Jerry S. Wolinski, M.D. from the University of Texas in Houston and George H. Kraft, M.D. from the University of Washington in Seattle as they worked their way down the list of potentially suitable prospective candidates to recruit to their respective institutions. I was very confused as to how I had landed on the radar of such spectacular clinicians and researchers. Out of fear of eventually disappointing them, I never actively pursued those leads. Despite my relative professional accomplishments, I felt insecure and that insecurity would continue to curse me in the ensuing few months as more job opportunities presented themselves.

We are told that when it rains, it pours, and it clearly was the case with regard to job opportunities. Within a matter of days, invitations for interviews rolled in one after another and I had the very difficult duty of learning as much as I could about the various opportunities to decide whether or not I would be interested in an on-site visit. A job opportunity came in from Arizona in an area that was so hot that it was recommended that dogs only be walked outside at sundown to avoid burning their paws. This, clearly, was a place Tallix and I had no interest in visiting. I decided to visit Macon, Georgia, a gorgeous city just over an hour south of Atlanta. The road to Macon was surrounded by pine trees and I felt as though I was driving through the Landes forest in Southwestern France. While the scenery between Bordeaux and Paris resembles Iowa, the scenery in central Georgia was identical to the scenery south of Bordeaux. I very much enjoyed the tour of the hospital as well as the tour of the community. Central

Georgia looks like an absolutely beautiful place to live and the people there are warm and welcoming.

After my visit to Macon, I visited Rapid City in South Dakota. The highlight of the surrounding area is of course Mount Rushmore which I had visited in the summer of 1995. In 2015 however, Mount Rushmore looked very different as a large cement infrastructure had been built at the site, in my opinion, taking away from the overall appeal as I enjoyed this phenomenal monument more when it was in its earlier, more natural state. Again, I liked the hospital tour and Sandra, Tallix and I also enjoyed the community tour which gave us a glimpse at where we could potentially live if we decided to move into the area. The people we met in South Dakota were lovely and we would have gotten along very well.

Soon after, I traveled to Reno, Nevada, to meet with Dr. James Lynch of SpineNevada to discuss an opportunity specifically in spinal cord medicine, not with his group, but with the main rehabilitation facility in Reno. I don't remember how exactly I ended up in contact with Dr. Lynch but assume that Dr. Brooks Rohlen might have been involved in helping us connect. Dr. Lynch is an ultra-energetic, exquisitely brilliant physician and entrepreneur of whom I was in awe from the first time we met. He is an incredibly accomplished and tremendously busy neurosurgeon who has a passion for helping people. He thought that my presence in Reno could be beneficial to improve local efforts to care for spinal cord injured patients. At this point however, while having a spinal cord injury myself, I was more an expert on Multiple Sclerosis. Dr. Lynch introduced me to the upper echelon of the hospital administration among whom, Dr. Anthony Slonim. Dr. Slonim is a quadruple board-certified physician by training, who has published over 120 publications and 15 textbooks and has an impressive track record of success both as a physician and a hospital administrator. I had actually read one of his books titled: "Manual of Healthcare Leadership: Essential Strategies for Physician and Administrative Leaders." I also met with the Medical Director of the Rehabilitation Hospital, Dr. Stefan Humphries, a retired American Football player who was part of the Chicago Bears when they won the Superbowl in 1985. After retiring from playing football, Dr. Humphries had enrolled at the University of Colorado School of Medicine and after graduation from medical school, completed a residency in Physical Medicine and Rehabilitation at the Mayo Clinic. During my visit to the Reno area, I stayed at Tim and Holly McGowan's house. Dr. Lynch, Dr. Humphries, Holly and I attended the Silver Tie Gala in support of the High Fives Foundation based in Truckee. According to its website, the mission of the High Fives Foundation is to support the dreams of outdoor action sport athletes by raising injury prevention awareness while providing resources and inspiration to those who suffer life-altering injuries. We had a fabulous time at the event. Obviously, I loved the Reno-Tahoe area, I had friends in the community, and had just been befriended by Dr. Lynch who, as previously mentioned, is a one of a kind individual and an unbelievably successful man. Despite all this, I didn't take the job in Reno and this missed opportunity is one of the biggest mistakes I made in my life. I often wondered why I didn't decide to take the job and found it difficult to come up with a reasonable and coherent answer. After much pondering, I realized that deep down, I felt intimidated. The opportunity looked too good to be true and I thought myself undeserving. Many years later, I learned of a condition called "Impostor Syndrome" which

I believe I suffered from, and from which I am still suffering. Impostor Syndrome is a psychological pattern in which individuals doubt their accomplishments and believe that their success is the result of luck and that others see them as more intelligent and deserving than they really are. This is precisely what happened to me and I felt insecure and couldn't envision myself in the company of such elite physicians, by fear that the shortcomings I believed I had would be exposed and I would ultimately be found wanting.

Finally, essentially out of the blue, I received a call from Salt Lake City where I had been recommended to take over a private Multiple Sclerosis clinic as the current Medical Director was looking to retire after a long and successful career in medicine. Working in MS, in Salt Lake City, seemed like an opportunity I couldn't turn down. I agreed to return to my "home-town of adoption" without even going for an on-site visit.

The last few months in Waterloo were emotionally charged because Sandra and I had grown to very much like the city and the precious friendships we had developed with our neighbors. We spent a lot of time hanging out with Marna and Jack who had us over frequently and had taken us under their wing and whom we considered as family. During the summer of 2015, while walking Tallix up an alley I had never gone up before, I met a charming woman named Audrey Porter. She invited me into her yard to meet her husband PJ. PJ and Audrey were land owners in the surrounding Reinbeck area and introduced me to the world of farming. Their son Clark took Sandra, Tallix and me on an educational tour of the farm and Sandra had an opportunity to ride in the combine, a humongous piece of machinery used in harvesting. We were very excited to learn plenty of interesting facts pertaining to the farming culture that is so prevalent in Iowa.

When it came time to move from Waterloo to Salt Lake City in the first week of October 2015, the move was not without tears.

CHAPTER 30

RETURN TO SALT LAKE CITY

Prior to arriving in Salt Lake City, with the help of my good friend Stefani Kimche, a realtor in the Park City area, I had purchased two condominiums, sight unseen. The first one was at the Stillwater Lodge on the western shore of Jordanelle Reservoir between Park City and Heber City and the other was in Salt Lake City not far from the MS clinic where I would work as the new Medical Director. Fred Langeland and his boys met us upon arrival to assist with the unloading of the moving truck. Within a day, Sandra had all the boxes put away and the place was taking shape as our new home.

Edonis, my sweet little rabbit turned 11 years old at the end of October 2015 which is unusually old for a rabbit of her breed. I want to believe that a diet consisting exclusively of organic products, a free roaming active lifestyle through the house and unconditional love from me played a big role in her long-lasting life. I had built little steps leading to the bed and whenever I laid down, she would run to lay next to me, under a fleece blanket, resting her head gently on my shoulder while I wrapped her body with my arm and rubbed her back with my hand for several hours each day. She was in rabbit heaven. During the day, she followed sun beams through the house as she enjoyed the warmth the sun provided. When the sun went down and I wasn't in bed, she enjoyed laying in front of the chimney.

For the first three years of my career in Waterloo, Sandra, Tallix and I only took one week of vacation to Key West so that I could go swim with Talon, the dolphin I had adopted at the Dolphin Research Center on Marathon Key. The rest of my vacation days from the hospital were spent traveling and lecturing on behalf of various pharmaceutical companies. As a result of this relentless work schedule, I had been able to completely pay off my educational loans pertaining to Brigham Young University and the University of Utah School of Medicine. With significant debt out of the way, I was free to flirt with perhaps less responsible ways to spend my hard-earned money and enjoy the fruits of my labor.

While in Medical School, my brother David and I joked that in the future, I might be able to own an Aston Martin if all went according to plan. Obviously, the original plan had been mangled amidst my life altering accident but the dream of owning an exotic car remained anchored in my mind, itself unaltered. I had been in love with Aston Martins ever since I saw the DBS that James Bond drove in Casino Royale. Interestingly, Dr. Lynch, himself a very charismatic man, also had an Aston Martin DBS, a car that elegantly matched his allure. The Aston Martin DBS was the perfect blend of aptitude and refinement and flawlessly embodied the characteristics of every Aston Martin: Power, Beauty and Soul. Being seated behind the wheel of a special vehicle made me forget about my paralysis as the wheelchair was essentially removed from the picture and I had always yearned to possess a nice car that could transiently allow me to escape reality. After extensively browsing the internet in search of my dream car, I happened to find one available for sale locally. On the day of my 41st birthday I visited the Ferrari dealership in Salt Lake City to look at an Aston Martin DB9 on display in the showroom. The beasty 6.0L V12 power unit was a far cry from the puny 1.3L 3cyl engine from the Geo Metro of yesteryears. My upbringing had not predisposed me to such extravagance, and my life's path had not been a straight forward shot toward success, but I felt, at that moment, after years and years of hard work, that perhaps I had earned the right to reward myself. I bought the car on the spot, happy birthday to me! The car was custom fitted with hand controls and might have been one of very few, if not the only hand-controlled Aston Martin in the world. On the day of delivery, Fred met me at the dealership so that he could drive my other car home. Prior to taking the Aston Martin on the winter roads, I wanted to ensure the dynamic stability control (DSC) was engaged by pressing on the DSC button on the dash until the light went on. This powerful car fitted with high performance summer tires turned out to be incredibly challenging to control on the cold slippery roads and Fred, who was following me, stated that the rear of the car shifted sideways upon each bout of acceleration off a traffic light. As it turned out, I had been naïve and later learned from the owner's manual that the DSC was always "on" by default and that the light was an indication that the DSC had been properly disabled to enable the driver to explore the vehicle to its limits, which, by the way, is never recommended on icy roads. I had erroneously assumed that the light meant that the dynamic stability control was turned on. For the first time in my life, I saw the need to carefully study the car's owner's manual in order to decipher how to properly operate this perhaps less than intuitive vehicle. Over the course of my ownership of this exotic grand tourer, I found that my heart rate increased every time I took it out of the garage, out of shear anxiety. Tallix didn't especially like the narrow rear bucket seats and the sloping roof line too low for his taste. While the car was technically big enough for Tallix, my wheelchair and I, it couldn't accommodate Sandra which earned me some negative reviews. When driving around with Sandra, we had to leave the wheelchair home. It was definitely a point A to point A car that was never used for anything other than just "enjoying" the driving experience. People commonly took out their phones to take pictures of it as we drove by and it was fun to answer questions about it while sitting at traffic lights or while refueling at the gas station, which had to be done frequently. Overall, to be fair, it must be said that it wasn't particularly comfortable and the suspension was so tightly sprung that it rattled the occupants when driving over the smallest of irregularities on the road surface. I joked that one would violently shake in the seat from driving over bird droppings. While I had managed to purchase my dream car, I received adverse votes from Sandra and Tallix who both preferred our other vehicle, an Audi A6 Avant Quattro which was clearly more functional. I was always worried that something bad might happen to the Aston Martin which was nerve wrecking, and I realized through experience that I did not own the car, but rather, it owned me. I also learned that sometimes we chase a dream, only to realize once it is reached, that it is in fact more of a nightmare that doesn't really fit in day-to-day life from a practical standpoint. Having almost learned my lesson, I traded the two-door exotic Aston Martin for a more practical and family friendly four-door Maserati Ghibli SQ4 which came with all-wheel drive and a set of snow tires and Sandra's seal of approval.

My work schedule was quite nice and while I worked 12 hours a day, I only worked 4 days a week as the Medical Director of the MS Clinic. I provided care exclusively to patients with Multiple Sclerosis, all day every day and continued working for the pharmaceutical industry to lecture throughout Utah and other western states. I spent a lot of effort on providing the best possible care I could to my patients and had time to write extensive and detail oriented clinical notes well delineating my thought process for the plan of care. A lot of patients were referred to me upon initial diagnosis, or to confirm the diagnosis of MS from the ophthalmology department at the University of Utah and I knew that my notes would be read by attending physicians whom I knew, and I wanted to ensure that they would be proud of the work I did after graduation.

Unfortunately, this return to Salt Lake City, initially fueled by high hopes, turned disastrous within a few months and 2016 was without a doubt the worst year in my life. On January 12th I came home after a long day at work to find Edonis, laid on her side, lifeless. Finding my baby inert on the floor, while inevitable, was a devastating blow. The next morning, as I took her little body, carefully wrapped in a fleece blanket to be cremated, I mentioned to the veterinarian that Tallix had looked more sluggish than usual over the prior couple of weeks. We had to return to the animal clinic at lunchtime for some x-rays and the first doctor told me that he suspected Tallix might have cancer and referred me to another veterinarian specializing in Oncology. My friend Jed accompanied me to the appointment later in the afternoon on January 13th where a lymph node biopsy was taken. The veterinarian explained that the high level of pollution, so prevalent in the Salt Lake

Valley due to a climatic effect known as "inversion" not infrequently caused lymphadenopathy in dogs with sensitive immune systems. He explained that there were also two types of lymphomas commonly seen in dogs, B-cell lymphoma which was curable and T-cell lymphoma which carried the most life-threatening prognosis. Having just lost Edonis, I was in a precarious emotional state and couldn't fully wrap my head around the possibility of losing my other best friend. Following Murphy's Law that if things can go wrong, they will, the blood sample which had been sent to the University of Colorado oncology department returned positive for T-cell Lymphoma. I was offered a course of treatment with a weak chance of success but was determined to do whatever I could for my boy, whatever the cost. I was asked to leave Tallix overnight for observation after receiving his first chemotherapy injection. Tallix and I had never been separated and it seemed absolutely unconceivable that we would spend the night apart. I was eventually talked into following the doctor's recommendation for Tallix's welfare. Over the ensuing few days, Jed came to the condo to help me give Tallix his oral meds. I learned through my own research that the life expectancy for T-cell lymphoma was around the two-week mark in the majority of cases and that dogs only rarely survived a year. Tallix and I spent every day at the animal clinic and it was gut wrenching to see tears rolling down my little bear's sweet face as they poked and probed him. I took him back to work with me where I laid with him in the CT scanner to evaluate how extensive the problem was. The imaging revealed swollen lymph nodes throughout the chest cavity. Tallix only derived mild benefits from the corticosteroids to shrink the nodes and I bought a plane ticket for Sandra to return from Germany on February 2nd so that she could spend time with us. On

February 4th, as he struggled to breathe, I called the veterinarian who came to our bedroom where I laid on the floor with Tallix, to help him cross the rainbow bridge. I held him in my arms my head against his chest, petting him, kissing him and talking to him when suddenly, I felt his heart stop.

Tallix and I had been a solid, inseparable unit for many years. He was my loving companion, my best friend and my protector. Tallix was an essential part of me and as he died, a part of me died with him.

Losing Edonis and Tallix in a three-week span seemed utterly unreal. They were everything to me. Every day after that, patients in the clinic, always used to seeing Tallix by my side, asked where he was and I had to explain what had happened, over and over, several times every day which was so incredibly difficult from an emotional standpoint. I spent the next few months in a complete haze, trying to focus on my work and finding no joy in any other aspect of my then depleted life.

Through Tallix's Facebook page, via mail and email, I received hundreds of condolences from people whom we had met through our travels and whose life he had touched. Many wrote about the impressions they had upon meeting him for the first time and in their own words referred to his quiet magnificence and regal character.

My nurse, in an effort to lift my spirits, took me to the Humane Society to look at adopting another companion to fill the void or at least provide some distraction and give back a sense of purpose to my life. As we were there, a foster parent brought in a 2-month old German Shepherd-Husky mix named Beatrix. I took her in my arms where she fell asleep. I adopted this little puppy and took her home to raise her. Jed, the clinic owner and the entire staff were very supportive of my efforts to raise a puppy from scratch which is, as I found out, very challenging and time-consuming. I wouldn't have been able to do it without their help.

In the wake of so much heartbreak, a page had to be turned to allow for some sort of emotional reboot to take place, to hopefully enable me to continue on with a life for which I had lost the taste.

CHAPTER 31

A EUROPEAN VACATION

In the spring of 2016, I realized that I had been so focused on growing my career that I had not made time to visit Europe in the previous 8 years. Sandra's family lived near Munster in Germany and I hadn't had a chance to meet her parents and grandmother yet. Sandra and I thus decided to travel to Germany and Spain to spend one week with her family followed by one week with mine. During our two-week absence, Beatrix Von Havixbeck went to boarding school with a professional dog trainer who specialized in training dogs for the police department. Her own dog, an athletic young German Shepherd named Ryker was a stunning and very able attack dog. Once, as we were walking Beatrix and Ryker around Echo Reservoir north of Coalville, Utah, a rope, 1 inch in diameter was dangling from the branch of a tree, some 6 feet off the ground. She told Ryker to jump and bite into the end of the rope. He instantly executed the command and sunk his teeth into the rope and swung from it until she told him to release. I was used to being the guy on the good side of an attack dog and sometimes had a hard time understanding how people could be afraid of Tallix, but seeing Ryker in action, it became evident to me how people could be intimidated by such an animal. Obviously, the goal for Beatrix was not to jump 6 feet to bite into the end of a rope, but rather to be well behaved and responsive off leash and Sandra and I were confident that this successful trainer could achieve our relatively modest goals.

Upon our arrival in Amsterdam, Sandra's father Peter picked us up and drove us to their home in Havixbeck where her mother Ingrid had prepared the most wonderful display of food I had ever seen for lunch. I also had the opportunity to meet her grandmother Grete and the family dog, Sandra's baby, Robbie, the cutest White West Highland Terrier who turned out to be a real cuddle bug. Sandra's parents were very accommodating and had acquired a foldable aluminum ramp for me to use over the few steps leading to our living quarters. While I remember not being able to communicate well due to the language barrier, I found her parents to be very kind.

The week in Westphalia was followed by a week in the resort town of Torrox Costa near Malaga in Spain where I flew my mother and my two nephews Alexandre and Quentin to meet us. My high-school friend Xavier was also able to join us for a few days.

Upon seeing my mother, I was impressed by how thin she looked. At a glance, I estimated her to weigh right around 100lbs which didn't seem healthy. The immediately noticeable hoarseness in her voice, combined with her significant smoking history and substantial weight loss meant one thing to me: She should be evaluated for laryngeal cancer without delay. She casually brushed off my recommendation, stating that her hoarse voice was only the result of a common cold from which she didn't seem to be able to recover. I knew her to always be quick to deny any negative effect that could come from cigarette smoking, so I wasn't entirely surprised by her initial reaction. She went on to explain, as absurd as it may sound, that in her fifty years of smoking, she never inhaled the smoke. I tried to use science and reason to explain how that wasn't possible, to no avail. I imagine that deep down, she was intelligent enough to comprehend that a lifelong history of heavy smoking was not entirely without consequences and she feared that I might be correct in my assumption.

We had a beautiful time together in Spain and spent most of our days at the pool but also went to the beach and Alexandre and Quentin carried me to the water so that I could swim. I was impressed by how little effort it took to float in the Mediterranean Sea because of its elevated salt content and subsequent high buoyancy and remember having had a hard time trying to get my head under water. For meals, we ate fresh sea food from the restaurants on the promenade. We endeavored to visit the surrounding area, including the towns of Competa and Nerja. Torrox Costa is well known for having the best climate in Europe and is a popular destination for pensioners from England and Germany seeking to spend their retirement in the sun. That plan to retire in the sun seemed like a very legitimate one to me, and the thought of eventually retiring there entered my mind.

Upon her return to France, my mom underwent an otolaryngologic evaluation, was diagnosed with laryngeal cancer and was scheduled for a course of radiation therapy to shrink the tumor near her vocal cords. Her appetite and ability to adequately swallow food declined amidst irritation and edema from the treatment and she would go on to lose more weight she couldn't truly afford to lose. Somehow, while definitely weakened, she continued to attend to her activities of daily living in the home, albeit while gradually requiring more assistance for the physically demanding tasks. Unfortunately, she was never able to quit smoking, even in the face of cancer and having been told unequivocally that radiation could only be done once and that smoking significantly increased her chance of tumor recurrence. When all is said and done, whether as medical professionals or as family members, all we can really do is educate people about the consequences of their actions and allow them to do what they will with that information. I cannot be angry at my mother for not changing a lifestyle that can be so destructive to her health. I can only educate her and love her no matter what path she chooses to follow.

Upon my own return to Salt Lake City, needing a change of environment in the aftermath of the recent sorrow that had befallen upon my immediate family, namely the consecutive deaths of Edonis and Tallix, I asked Sandra where she would like to move. She answered that Iowa had been good to us and that perhaps we should make our way back there. There was no need for me in Waterloo from a professional standpoint and after a quick internet search, Sandra found a position for me in Davenport in Eastern Iowa on the Mississippi river. The hospital there was looking to fill a position exclusively on the inpatient rehabilitation unit. I would not have the responsibilities of a Medical Directorship on my shoulders and would only fill the position of a regular staff physiatrist. As I evaluated this prospect, I thought the probable change of pace would be beneficial to me, at least for a little while, as I healed my emotional wounds.

Toward the end of our time in Salt Lake City, my uncle Patrick came to spend a month of vacation with us during which period we spent a pleasant week-end in an old cabin in the Bryce Canyon National Park. The following week-end, we drove to Promontory Summit to visit the Golden Spike National History Site where, on May 10th, 1869, the Union and Central Pacific Railroads joined their rails and the Jupiter and No. 119 steam locomotives came face to face, marking the completion of the nation's first transcontinental railroad.

    Following my uncle's departure, my dad flew in from France to help with the move back to Iowa.

CHAPTER 32

DAVENPORT

We planned a leisurely pace to reach Davenport, Iowa in three days. Heading east on I-80 from Park City, Utah, we spent the first day driving through Wyoming. The second day, we drove through Nebraska, and finally, the third day we drove through Iowa and arrived in Davenport under a foot of snow, right on time for the first snow storm of the season.

While crossing Iowa, we had the opportunity to stop in Winterset to see the tiny home where John Wayne was born on May 26th, 1907 under the name of Marion Mitchell Morrison. Never in my wildest dreams had I ever thought, while watching country western movies in my youth, that I would one day visit the birthplace of John Wayne.

During our very first evening in Davenport, while getting settled in the hotel room, I received a call from Dr. Lynch who informed me that Dr. Stefan Humphries had decided to move down to Arizona to work at the Mayo Clinic in Scottsdale and proceeded to inquire about my availability to move to Reno. Had he called only a few weeks before, my answer would have been a resounding

"Yes!" unfortunately, having just signed an employment contract and having just arrived in Davenport, the situation was more complex. I was painfully torn between the inner desire to go to Reno and the desire to do the right thing with respect to my contract. Of course, contracts can be broken, but I had just signed a one-year lease for an apartment in Davenport, I didn't yet have a license to practice Medicine in Nevada and mentally, I had made myself comfortable with the idea of spending some time in the Midwest enjoying a slower pace of life. I asked my dad for his advice and he told me that a man is only as good as his word and I should honor my contract. As much as I knew I would perhaps come to regret it, I turned down the offer yet again.

I didn't start work until January 2017 and we had the entire month of December to familiarize ourselves with the Quad City area which, we were told, was twice as nice as the Twin Cities. It must be said that Iowa tends to be more charming in the springtime than it is in winter and my dad was impressed by the low temperatures. One day, we drove to Galena, Illinois where the temperature was -30 F (-34 C) and my dad said that he had never experienced this type of weather before at any point in his life. To keep ourselves entertained, we visited a few local museums, among which, the Iowa 80 Trucking Museum in Walcott, Iowa which has a stunning display of beautifully restored historical and one-of-a-kind trucks. We also visited the John Deere combine manufacturing plant, the John Deere Headquarters and the John Deere Pavilion in Moline, Illinois. We learned about the history of this impressive company and the various innovative pieces of equipment that it produces.

Up the Mississippi river, we traveled a short distance to LeClaire, Iowa, birthplace of William Frederick

"Buffalo Bill" Cody on February 26th, 1846, and current home of the Buffalo Bill Museum and Antique Archaeology, an antique store featured on the History Channel's reality television series, American Pickers. The Buffalo Bill Museum presents interesting artifacts including a wonderful display of the Lone Star, a 105ft wooden paddlewheel steam-powered towboat built in 1868, which has been declared as a National Historic Landmark.

During our time in the Quad Cities, we had a chance to dine on the Mississippi river aboard the Celebration Belle, a 750-passenger vessel built by Patti Shipbuilding of Pensacola, Florida. I also had the opportunity to ride my handcycle while pulling Beatrix in the trailer on the edge of the Mississippi.

Sandra and I had somehow been under the impression that it was necessary for us to wait until I was granted citizenship from the United States before we could get married, and I wasn't eligible to apply for citizenship for the first 5 years as a green card holder. Once we realized that we had been mistaken and could get married whenever we wished, we opted to get married in the spring of 2018 without further delay.

CHAPTER 33
A WEDDING CELEBRATION

Sandra called the Havixbeck city hall to inquire about the availability of the chapel at the water castle of Burg Hulshoff and the wedding date was set for June 15th, 2018. The castle, situated amidst sumptuous grounds and surrounded by a pond, had been the residence of 19th century German poet and composer Annette von Droste-Hulshoff.

Having family and friends in different countries, we knew it would be impossible to get everybody to attend a single reception. Therefore, after some deliberation and for the convenience of our guests, we opted to have three receptions in three countries. The first reception would take place in Havixbeck, Germany on the evening of the wedding itself. Another reception would take place in Bordeaux, France a few days later, and finally, a third one would take place in Salt Lake City. Fred and Shirley Langeland traveled to all three receptions and Chris and Amanda Langeland traveled to Germany to attend the wedding and the first reception.

While it rained very hard the afternoon before the wedding, we were blessed with gorgeous weather on the wedding day. All of Sandra's family and her closest friends were in attendance. After a multilingual ceremony in the private chapel attached to the castle, we shared a wedding cake on top of which unusual figurines of the groom and bride had been set. Unlike the usually encountered standing groom and bride, I was pleased to discover that our figurines were both in the seated position which was a very nice touch. After the customary wedding pictures on the castle's grounds, we had a succulent dinner at the Steverburg restaurant with all our German guests.

We then flew to Bordeaux where we enjoyed marvelous weather. The day before the reception, Fred, Shirley, Sandra and I met with my younger brother Geoffrey for a tour of the city. I felt as though I was a genuine tourist in my own city and admired the magnificent buildings and their architecture with almost a naïve perspective because it had been so long since my prior visit. Bordeaux is truly a breathtaking city. Determined to eat good food while in France, we ate lunch at one of Gordon Ramsay's Michelin-starred restaurants, Le Pressoir d'Argent. Later the same day, I had reserved the private dining room at another Michelin-starred restaurant, La Table d'Hotes, Le Quatrieme Mur, where celebrated French Chef Philippe Etchebest and his crew entertain a very limited number of guests in an intimate stone walled room in prolongation of the kitchen underneath Le Grand Theatre de Bordeaux. True to form and as expected for this caliber of fine dining, the entire experience lasted over 4 hours with the first course being brought out at 8pm and the last bite of dessert taking place after midnight. It was a memorable experience I was happy to share with my dad, his wife Brigitte, my brother Geoffrey, Fred, Shirley and Sandra. The next day, we hosted my family and friends at a reception at the Comptoir de Seze. It was a very emotional moment for me to see, at once, so many family members and friends I had not had the opportunity to see in a long time. As determined as I was to offer a meaningful toast, I found myself with a lump in my throat, unable to hold back tears within the first few words when I realized through saying it at loud, how long I had been away. "Ten years have passed already since my last visit…" How unforgivable! Sandra and I agreed to make a particular effort to, from then on, travel to France at least once a year to visit family. People do not get any younger and the time that has passed and the moments that have been missed can never be recovered.

Toward the end of summer, we hosted the final reception which we dubbed a renewal of the vows in the orchard of the charming William Atkin Home located within This is The Place Heritage Park in Salt Lake City, where a catered dinner was served to our American guests. A lot of the people mentioned in this book were in attendance. Once again, we enjoyed a stunning weather. When most people hope to have nice weather for their wedding reception, we were blessed to have blue skies for all three of ours.

I was incredibly touched and humbled that so many people across three countries had honored us with their presence to celebrate my union to Sandra.

Overall, the organization of the wedding was associated with a significant amount of stress and it was, amidst the preparatory stages, difficult to see the light at the end of the tunnel. Even as the wedding was taking place, I was overtaken by worries about whether or not the event would go as planned. Such concerns and anxiety somehow lessened the enjoyment I should have derived from the moment in real time. It was only after the fact, as I had an opportunity to reflect on the meaning of my union to Sandra, that I fully realized what a lucky man I am to have had the chance not only to meet the perfect woman, but to marry her as well. Sandra has been a catalyst for my happiness and the work she does behind the scenes, the encouragement and support she continually provides, have allowed me to be happier and more productive than I could ever have been without having her in my life.

CHAPTER 34

PENSACOLA

While Davenport was a nice place to live with a mellow lifestyle and very supportive people, the harsh winter conditions generally present in Iowa over several months each year made me consider relocating to a warmer, more wheelchair-friendly climate. Winter had become progressively more depressing due to the limitations it placed on someone requiring the use of a wheelchair. Shoveling one's way through 2 feet of snow is definitely a young man's game. Over time, I had become less tolerant of the cold and had grown more concerned about the complications sub-zero temperatures and massive amounts of snow could potentially add to my life. At the time, in the context of Sandra and I both being interested in spending more time with our respective families, I was prepared to retire from medicine and move to southern Spain should it be needed.

In August 2018, my medical school friend, Dr. Aaron Waite, a successful corneal surgeon with a thriving practice in Lehi, Utah, offered to perform corrective surgery on my eyes so that I would no longer need to rely on glasses which had started to cause headaches when worn extensively over my long work days. He explained that poor vision is a disability, but a disability that could fortunately be cured thanks to modern technology and he would be honored to have the privilege to help me perfect my vision so that I would only have to deal with one disability and not two. I was very touched by this message and agreed that correcting my vision would be undeniably beneficial. In October 2018, Sandra, Beatrix and I flew back to Salt Lake City and I underwent corrective corneal surgery. Being once again on the patient side of the doctor-patient relationship, I was very impressed by Aaron's ability to positively affect my life and was grateful for the time and effort he had dedicated to the learning and the perfecting of his craft. Aaron not only improved my vision, through his example, he also helped me see the type of success and personal gratification I could continue to enjoy if I kept pushing forward to improve other people's conditions in life. I reflected on the impact that I hopefully had in my own patients' lives and realized that there was room for a lot of good yet to be done. I was instilled with the desire to seek ways through which I could continue to expand my reach and help more patients suffering from functional disabilities. As I pondered my particular situation, I was reminded that my condition was beneficial to my disabled patients as it allowed them to see, in me, the potential they could reach in their own recovery. The expansive reward that comes from helping others tremendously adds to the happiness one can experience in life and perhaps it was too early for me to retire as I still had something to contribute. Consequently, instead of hanging my hat just yet, Sandra and I looked for opportunities through which I could continue to benefit the patient population I had dedicated my professional career to serving, albeit in a warmer climate. I took a leap of faith! In order to make myself available for new potential life opportunities, I gave my resignation to my employer. Immediately after, as often happens when the universe conspires to make one's dreams come true, I was invited to investigate a couple of employment opportunities in the Florida Panhandle. After visiting the Emerald Coast and being offered a very exciting position with a lot of potential for professional growth, we decided to relocate to this more clement part of the country to continue my medical endeavors.

Fred and Shirley flew in from Salt Lake City to help with the move and on February 28th, 2019, we started our journey south. We opted to take it slow and split the 980-mile drive into three manageable sections, spending the first night in Saint Louis, Missouri, the second in Birmingham, Alabama, to finally reach Pensacola on the third day.

March 4th, 2019 marked the thirteen-year anniversary of my accident. The next day, I started working as the new Medical Director of the renowned West Florida Rehabilitation Institute in Pensacola, the largest rehabilitation facility in the Florida Panhandle. This new stimulating opportunity would allow me to further my quest to lose myself in the care of patients suffering from functional and mobility deficits secondary to strokes, traumatic brain injuries, spinal cord injuries, limb amputations or other complicated and disabling medical illnesses. Helping others find ways to overcome their disabilities as I have overcome my own, is my passion, and I feel ever so blessed for the chance I have to be involved in such important and meaningful work.

CHAPTER 35

LAST WORDS

When playing any card game, success is at least in part dependent on the initial haphazard distribution of cards. Some get an advantageous hand while others do not. That random assignment of cards is only partly responsible for the overall outcome of each game and it is best not to dwell on what cannot be changed and instead, to push forward until a better selection comes, and strive always to play the best hand available, or better yet, to force one's luck through acquiring a mastery of the rules and through dedicated practice.

Similarly, in life, one needs to study ways that lead to success regardless of initial circumstances. The famous business guru Brian Tracy states that to achieve success, one needs to follow the recipe of other successful people. There is no need to reinvent the wheel. Instead of spending time coming up with my own recipe for success, I have intuitively patterned my entire life after people I admired, and whose paths I wanted to follow and whose lives I wanted to emulate.

The next time you encounter a gloomy situation, think to yourself: How can I make something good out of this? Always keep your head up and focus on what the opportunities can be. While it is easy, and initially necessary to contemplate and mourn what isn't there, what has been lost, or the missed prospects in any situation, it is much more valuable to focus on and cherish what is left and look forward to the opportunities yet to come.

I was not born in what can be considered an especially advantageous environment, but I developed impeccable work ethics and made up for this lack of advantage by creating my own opportunities. Along the way, I have lost the use of my legs, but I still have my arms and my brain, and I owe it to myself and to those who believe in me and who continue to support me throughout the years, to make the best of what I have.

Make the best of what you have, play your best hand because that is all you can do, and the rest will sort itself out.

I am reminded of the saying commonly attributed to John Lennon that life is what happens to us while we are busy making other plans. Sometimes it is necessary to acknowledge the fact that unexpected events serve to allow our destiny to reveal itself. The quest for the silver lining of any cloud can be a rewarding one. My personal accident helped define my purpose within medicine by delineating my calling in life. No profession and no medical specialty would have suited me better than a career as a physician in the field of Physical Medicine and Rehabilitation, which I stumbled upon, accidentally, as life was showing me the way.

Along my somewhat tumultuous journey, I have allowed outside influences, sometimes intentionally sought after and occasionally unplanned for, to infiltrate my life and change it for the better.

I am eternally grateful to all those who have played a supporting role in my life and never forgot where I came from or the care and guidance that I received along the way, which enabled me to get to where I am today.

In the pursuit of my American Dream I have been blessed with opportunities to cross paths with many phenomenal, positively influential people who have all left an indelible impact on the course of my life and have allowed me to fulfill a potential I did not know I had.

During one of our many privileged conversations, Larry H. Miller told me to go about doing good in the world until there is too much of it. I am doing my best to follow this wise advice and want to end this humble book by echoing Larry's words and urging you, dear reader, to go about doing the same.

Epilogue

By SANDRA YONNET

If we equate the pursuit of a purpose, the chase of a goal in life, to the climbing of a mountain, and compare the ascent to the summit with its turns and forks and long stretches to the challenges one has to face and the obstacles one has to overcome before reaching the summit, we find that while there is no sure formula for success, perseverance, and undying motivation make an essential contribution.

Goals give meaning to our existence. We all have goals and we all try our best to reach them. Sometimes the initial target changes or we settle down earlier than anticipated because we found contentment somewhere along the way. And sometimes unforeseeable occurrences, or even tragedies strike, unraveling our world and shaking our faith to the very core. When this happens, we must choose to either surrender to despair or find the strength to pick ourselves back up and reassess our options to make the best of the situation.

My husband was "climbing a mountain" when he got hit by an avalanche right before reaching the summit.

This avalanche not only stopped him abruptly in his tracks, it threw him downhill with a force he had never before experienced. The impact broke his spine and took away the use of his legs, but it did not knock the fight out of him, it did not break his spirit. He couldn't climb the last portion of the journey through the use of his legs and instead of gently sliding back to the bottom of the hill, he pushed forward and reached the summit with the use of his arms.

His strong will fueled the stamina and courage necessary to get back up and keep going, almost unperturbed. I am amazed to see all he was able to accomplish and overcome in life despite knocks that would have left many out for the count. He tells me that it is difficult to fathom what one can do until given no other choice and that most people can achieve much more than they think when their back is against the wall. Truly, he did have a choice, he just always chose to fight because to him, the choice of giving up doesn't exist.

My husband is the kind of person who immediately catches peoples' attention when he enters a room. He jokes that he "stands out" because of the wheelchair but I know that it is his personality that captivates. On first impression the truth can likely be found as a combination of both. The way he handles his wheelchair with ease, elegantly, makes it easy to forget it altogether and to simply be fascinated by his positive attitude and personal strength.

It is not the exemplary way he deals with his disability that defines him, it is his ability to move on from setbacks and continue to always push forward, steadfastly.

I am grateful to have found my place at his side and to love and be loved by this exceptional man.

Printed in Poland
by Amazon Fulfillment
Poland Sp. z o.o., Wrocław